A Guide for Those
the Symptomatic S

Teaching

Learning

Communities

Routines and Rituals for What

Teachers

Should

Know

And Be Able

To Do

For

Students

TEACHING LEARNING COMMUNITIES

A Guide for Those Who Care About Solving the
Symptomatic Solutions in Schools

ROUTINES & RITUALS

Eze Aso

TABLE OF CONTENTS

SECTION I

PRESUMPTIONS OF SOCIAL CHANGE IN EDUCATION

SECTION II

LEARNING COMMUNITY AND ACHIEVEMENT GAP

APPLICATION I

PROFESSIONAL PRACTICE IN STRATEGIC
SOCIETAL DEVELOPMENT

SECTION III

THEORIES OF HUMAN DEVELOPMENT AND
EDUCATION

APPLICATION III

PROFESSIONAL PRACTICE IN EDUCATION
ORGANIZATIONS

PREAMBLE

SECTION I

Theorists such as Dewey, Adler, Greene, and Apple have delineated how social change can be an important factor in society. Therefore, it is important to describe the dynamics of change and the implications of these changes for societal improvement. The theoretical perspectives discussed in this section will emphasize the rationale underlying societal change. Topics discussed in relation to theories of social change include democracy and education, community development and growth, the concept of freedom, individual freedom and society, contributions to education, and education and culture.

SECTION II

To close the achievement gap between African American, Hispanic American, and European American students places significant demands on the school community. These demands include how adults and professionals in educational settings perform duties and responsibilities that affect student learning. In this section, the component will examine current research on this topic in order to analyze the relationship of teaching to diversity and the impact of this relationship on the academic achievement gap between African America, Hispanic American and European American students. The achievement gap is as a construct that is defined in terms of its social implications. Therefore, this section will also describe current research related to administrative perceptions about the achievement gap, characteristics of learning communities, and the socio-economic status of the family.

APPLICATION I
The future academic success of students relies on the ability of the educational organization to be cognizant of the many facets of social change in education and the community. The achievement gap can be viewed in terms of social experience, behavior, and interaction. This component will explore current societal issues affecting the educational system as it relates to the African American and Hispanic American students. The project will describe methods of research that are utilized to evaluate, implement change and incorporate strategic planning for educators and policy makers. Recommendations for narrowing the achievement gap between African American, Hispanic American, and European American students are also included.

SECTION III
The section component will analyze and compare and contrast the theories of Piaget, Bandura, and Egan. Additionally, this will examine and describe the theorists' contributions to education today, particularly in relation to student achievement in American public schools. The section also includes a discussion

about how these theories contribute to the organization of educational systems. Major themes from each theorist about the role that children and adolescent cognitive development plays in promoting academic achievement for public school students at the secondary level is also discussed.

SECTION IV
The uncertainty surrounding the reason why cognitive discrepancy occurs may add to the difficulty in understanding human development. Therefore, this section will present a related literature review thesis that will examine current research in relation to the cognitive development of children and adolescents. The literature review paper will present current research studies on cognitive development as well as on the role of personality traits, locus of control (LOC), neighborhoods, schools, and culture in relation to cognitive development.

APPLICATION II
This section focuses on the habits of mind; habits of mind are qualities students need for managing uncertain or challenging situations while they are in high school. The application will describe 16 habits-of-mind strategies that students can use in a high-school environment. This application project may be useful in assisting educators to develop policies and effective teaching strategies that could contribute to improving high school graduation rates. Improving high school graduation rates

could improve college attendance, which in turn encourages the broad concepts, theories, and life perspectives of those students who attend college. College graduates add positive benefits to their communities.

SECTION V
The section involves a critical evaluation of the system thinking and theory of social systems theory. Attentions were given to the work of Peter Senge, Hoy & Miskel and Margaret Wheatley. The set-up for this component will involve a presentation of each of these system thinkers with an explanation and analysis of their significant contributions to organizational development, such as in educational system. The focus of this study is the historical development of each type of system studied; including, education, corporations, and government organizations. In addition, the different systems theories will be compared and contrasted in order to discuss the characteristics of each theory. However, the emphasis of this project is the contribution of the work of the preceding theorists in today's school system.

SECTION VI
The philosophy of systems theory and organization learning can be vital in changing the depressing productivity and academic achievement in science education today. Educational systems, such as science teachers and their classroom must look beyond traditional structures and model scientific

learning that work. Academic progression in the science education today is not functioning at the pace of changing technologies. Some underlining reasons for this state of stagnation could be accredited to the lack of effective and efficient instructional techniques in science. Empirical studies reveal that inquiry based lessons plays an important part in giving science classrooms the advancement on student science achievement. The main idea of this section is to increase student motivation and student achievement in biology course. Science frameworks, instructional strategies, and motivation will be discussed as a means to increase student interest and achievement in biology education.

APPLICATION III
The application part of this paper involves a project that utilizes the theoretical knowledge acquired in the section V and VI components with the subject specific to the lack of variety of instructional techniques resulting in poor biology academic performance in public schools. The other part of this component will be a scholarly written commentary of approximately 10 pages in length. In addition, the focus will be on the plan for a system change in science frameworks. This plan will include a professional development conducted with the principal and science teachers who will serve as the clients for this project application. The results of this systems approach to solving the problem of effective instructional techniques in science

education resulting in lack of motivation and interest in science will be forwarded to the science teachers for ongoing discussion and possible implementation.

ACKNOWLEDGEMENT

To my wife, Oluchi, and to my children, Anuri (JOY), Ebube, and Ekele, for enduring with me the many challenges that this experience has brought, thank you. In addition, I would like to thank my students present and past for a lesson well learned; I will keep cheering encouraging you through your academic quest.

SECTION I

PRESUMPTIONS OF SOCIAL CHANGE, FOUR THEORISTS

Many scholars are aware that the social theories of Dewey, Greene, Apple, and Adler have contributed to the changes and progress of education today. Several of the ideas that came out of their social theories involve education, community growth, and democracy. John Dewey (1915) believed that there is a strong relationship between social change and education. Dewey argued that K-12 educational institutions are tyrannical and prevent the growth and exploration of students. He insists that schools need to change; thus, he helped lead the reforms that made schools into institutions that allow students to develop free personalities. Dewey's ideas were put into practice in 1896 at University of Chicago Experimental School. Dewey's philosophy emphasized the impact of education on young adults and how they perceive his or her world from the knowledge acquired at school. Dewey believed that at school students should play a significant role in decisions that affect their learning. He was also concerned about the autonomy of teachers. Dewey also believed that learning could be accomplished by using real life tasks and challenges. He despised the unnecessarily long hours of school and its restrictiveness.

Greene (1995) believes, on the other hand, that educators should teach to the power of imagination. She believes that American education lacks imagination, supports provincial ideas, refuses to engage in social movements such as Civil Rights, and refuses to listen to the voices of other minority groups such as African American and Hispanic American students. Greene believes that moving education away from an intellectual exercise to one that falls under the wings of cultural criticism will improve school system. In order to accomplish this task, Greene suggests using theater, film, music, and novels as means into new ways of seeing and feeling. Furthermore, Greene claims that in order to see what should be done right, the need to learn from the events of the 1930s and 1960s is critical. She depolarizes and criticizes the system for being myopic to the changes of time, which she refers to as a one-dimensional worldview and a lack of ability to imagine alternatives realities. Consequently, Greene despises the use of testing and tracking and the tendency of treating education as a washed up profession. These attitudes lead teachers to discourage students to use their imaginations and to drilling students to produce the right answers on a test. Greene believes that freedom not only consist of choice, but "there has to be a space wide enough for you to resist what stands in the way of choice" (Greene, 1965, p. 124). Finally, Greene's contribution to educational change is her idea that educators need to invent a more vivid vision of the future in order to amend the deficiencies of the present.

Apple (2000) believes that educational institutions do not provide or teach students about democracy and equality, concepts that a civil society deserves. He claims that schools should be observed closely and scrutinized in relation to how they help individuals get ahead, and what kind of people actually get ahead by formulating problems that affect students. Consequently, Apple believes that schools produce an unequal society. In other words, society reproduces itself by governing autocratically, creating marginalization and equity issues, and thereby creating inferior social order. Furthermore, Apple focuses his attention on the government as a conservative branch, which attempts to change education through means of commercialization, privatization, standardization, and a return to past or to a more traditional system of education. Apple's emphasis is to show how the conservatives are radically changing society's ideas about what education is and whom it should serve. Apple's contribution to social change is his strong critique of the conservative right in educational policies and his ability to document the daily efforts of educators' struggles to accomplish a democratic process in the United States of America.

Adler (1902) insists that the demand for quality education in public schools is the only way to insure its survival. He claims that when schools separate students based on ability, schools have failed in their purpose to instill in its citizens a democratic system. In addition,

3

Adler believes that schools tend to achieve quantity rather than quality for all. This failure is a violation of democratic principles. Moreover, Adler believes that there is hypocrisy in the educational system. He claims that educational leaders including teachers preach the need to educate all citizens; however, in reality, educators give the opportunity of education to only the privileged few. Adler also strongly believes that "there are no un-teachable children. There are only schools and teachers and parents who fail to teach them" (p. 8). Adler made it clear that the teaching of a child should not be left solely to the school and that parents and the community at large need to step up and involve in the education of a child. Adler's major contribution to educational change was his belief in the need to increase the amount of time that children are in school. Adler also developed **The Paideia Proposal**, which is an educational manifesto that is still used in many of the public schools today.

Therefore, this sub-section will explore some of the theories of social change that have influenced the field of education. Theorists, such as Dewey, Adler, Greene and Apple have each described how social change can be an important factor in society. Therefore, it is important to describe the dynamics of change and the implications of these changes for societal improvement. The theoretical perspectives discussed in this sub-section will emphasize the rationale underlying societal development. Topics discussed include democracy and education, community development and growth, the concept of freedom, individual freedom and society, contributions to education, and education and culture.

Democracy and Education

Dewey (1915) believes that society is built on self-renewal. Educating members of the community who are immature brings about this self-renewal. This educational process is accomplished by various agencies, including the school community. It is well known in the present governance of American society that education is very important and necessary to sustain democratic processes. Equally important is the role that democracy plays in education. In relation to democracy and education, Dewey (1915) delineates education as the "reconstruction or reorganization of experience which adds to the meaning of experience and which increases the ability to direct the course of subsequent experience" (p. 6). Education like democracy is the basis of empowerment. In a simple way, education and democracy provide the necessary means to create, shape, and direct experience.

In a democratic system such as the United States, the most autocratic classrooms and institutions are led by the concept of basic freedom. If these freedoms are not found in these classrooms, they survive beyond them. The most important freedoms are the ability to choose a cause of action, the ability to act on the action chosen, and the opportunity to gain an experience as a result of this freedom of choice. For example, if a student chooses to enroll in a technical school rather than a college, the experience and the outcome of that experience is entirely up to the student, rather than the teachers or his or her parents, concerning the freedom to choose. According to John Dewey (1915), the idea of making choices and accepting the outcome of that choice helps a student to gain experience that could lead to other experiences, beliefs, and an understanding of the world and how it works and how humans thrive in a community.

Furthermore, John Dewey (1915) defined formal education as a process in which a society transfers its culture and beliefs to the next generation, in terms of its present day educational system and the achievement gap among students of different backgrounds. Could it be possible to assume that in a country such as the United States of America, there are many cultures that the schools have not embraced or assimilated in the day-to-day activities of the schools that have led to an achievement gap in relation to these cultures? In the United States, the only culture that the school system uses for teaching and learning tends to lean towards European cultures, and there is no room for other cultures. It seems that any other cultures brought by non-European students are often labeled, as learning disabled or special needs students. If John Dewey's idea of education is as a means to transfer culture and beliefs from one generation to another, then the present school system in the United States does a poor job of teaching students how to learn. For example, the curriculums in school today are focused on the next class or on academic work completed for the next grade; these curriculums are not allowing students to make choices, to act on those choices, and to perhaps have a wonderful experience that could motivate students for the next choice or idea. Hence, students will be served better if they are allowed to choose their course of study with minimal direction. At least when students enter a high school of choice, their academic needs should be tailored to the talents they possess for determining a career.

Maxine Greene (1965) believes that democracy is a very big part of a community. This community, according to her, is always evolving, full of camaraderie, with all people sharing some type of specific beliefs as well as a discourse about the wellness of others. Greene also discusses the community's ability to accommodate others from diverse backgrounds, mostly those individuals whom society has forgotten. Greene's (1965) theory of democracy seems appropriate to accommodate diverse groups of people, but does not explain what is happening in our current society. This democracy is evident in the management, teaching, and learning that transpire in the school community. What makes Greene's theory of democracy convincing is that it sounds realistic and appropriate for a workable, successful community where exploitation, competition, and social injustice do not exist.

Greene's theory of democracy was built from the ideas and visions of the founding fathers of democracy in the United States. However, when these ideas were developed, the founding fathers probably did not imagine the change in demography of the citizens that comprise the United States. Thus, those original ideas sounded appealing but could not accommodate our ever-changing present society. For example, the democratic process described by Greene or Dewey (1915) cannot account for the increase in the number of minorities getting educated or assuming leadership roles in such places as the educational system or the corporate world.

Nonetheless, Greene (1965) believes that the dominant force in managing educational issues comes from the officials who run the educational institutions. According to Greene, in these systems, management is a top-down way of thinking, in which teachers and students are not included in the process of educational management. According to Greene, the only role these groups play is to comply and serve. Observing the present-day school system managerial process, one can agree wholeheartedly with Greene's theory. The set up of school management structure can be traced back a few years when the "factory model" of placing students in rows and teaching them the same thing over and over, just to master the basics in order to get by was the norm. During these periods, this factory model was factored into the educational system in order to accommodate society's economic needs.

However, the changes in technology affected the economic needs of our present day society; schools have been trying to make changes to meet our changing society due to an increased demand in the technology sector. Nonetheless, these changes have forced changes in curriculum, special education, the classroom environment, and the instructional process of teachers, but they do not seem to transform how the school systems are governed. If changes need to happen in the schools, these changes should start with modifying how schools are governed. Special emphasis needs to focus on changing the "top-down" management mentality to "bottom-up" or allowing all stakeholders of a school including parents, students and teachers be part of the school management that still exists in schools. After all, teachers, students, and parents are in the forefront of the educational structure. Hence, they need to play an active role in the day-to-day management of the schools.

Michael Apple's theory (1993) elaborates on the reasons for educational failure in the school system; he believes that today teachers and other educators control school policy, practice, and implementation; however, this theory does not seem accurate, especially if one is an educator. Actually, this theory by Apple does not explain why many parents, who are supposedly stakeholders in the educational system and members of the community, participate in school activities when their children are young. Parents seem to be completely out of touch with schools when the child is much older. The policies and practices that guide the elementary schools are also present in middle school and high schools. When parents and the community do not seem to support school activities, teachers and other educators fill the void. For example, the school improvement team (SIT) is an organization formed by many schools to help in the development of school policies and practices. Parents and members of the communities, including business people, are encouraged to participate. However, most of the time, teachers and the rest of the professional educators end up populating and running the meetings. Many state departments of education mandate that schools have a standing SIT. Thus, educators must carry out meetings and school plans, whether parents and the communities participate or not. On the other hand, if parents and the community take charge within their neighborhood schools, become active participants in the school improvement team (SIT), or create strong parent teacher organizations (PTO), there will be no complete control of policy and practice as suggested by Michael Apple. Furthermore, parents and the communities will also be able to hold teachers and other educators, such as the principal and the superintendent, accountable for educating all students.

Michael Apple's (1993) theory of the old system of schooling traditions (chalk and talk) that dominate present-day schools has failed to accommodate and educate those who are marginalized by poverty, race, gender, and sexuality. Since the desegregation of schools and the influx of the new immigrants, the demographics of the student body in schools have changed and are still changing; more and more different cultural groups of students are now attending schools. However, the school systems are not changing to embrace the rich culture brought by the new immigrants to the school system. For example, when a non-European child enters the school system in kindergarten, chances are that the child has not been read to or even seen a book before; the child will struggle with literacy which forms the major part of the school culture. However, the school does not think about the child's culture, which is the primary venue at home before he or she attends school. In the process of acclimatizing to the new culture, the child may perform poorly in comparison to other children. Thus, the teacher gets frustrated, and the child may be labeled learning disabled or slow which results in the child dropping out of school early. The only dominant system still visible in American schools is the system that was developed by individuals of European descent. To be able to educate all students or to provide equity in schools, the school leaders, policy makers, and teachers need to involve many different kinds of cultures before introducing the main educational culture to students of different cultural backgrounds. Michael Apple's theory of the tradition that has been the dominating

11

power in the schools seems proper. The change in this tradition will help close the achievement gap between European American students and other non-European students. However, Michael Apple does address the issue of changing the traditional system of education to accommodate all students, but failed to describe the steps needed to accomplish this change.

Mortimer Adler's (1902) theory of educational equality for all students seems appropriate, but not practical. Adler's theory does not explain what transpires in school systems today. Adler's (1902) theory seems reasonable because it is persuasive. For example, Adler explains how education leads to democracy and how democracy is designed for free citizens who can choose to live comfortably as long as they do not infringe on other people's rights to live freely. Adler's theory of educational equality is not practical. Since the passage of the 1954 Supreme Court decision known as Brown vs. the Board of Education, which intended to eliminate segregation in schools, present day schools have still not removed segregation. For instance, school districts across the United States still maintain some type of segregation in their schools, such as gifted programs, advanced placement programs, or fast tracks as well as special education programs.

Community Development and Growth

John Dewey (1930) discusses the issue of human habits of the mind. According to Dewey, the most difficult challenge for humans in a society is controlling the need to form habits of minds that accommodate an ever-changing society in comparison to habits that restrict and limit responses to social challenges or changes in society. The issue concerning habits of the mind is that these habits may confine or liberate decision-making and reactions to a situation. Habits of the mind may limit a person's thinking about a situation for which actions and behaviors are not beneficial. For example, in an educational environment, testing is the norm; however, this testing can lead to frequent drill and kill methods of learning.

Dewey (1930) believes that habits of the mind may liberate human thinking and problem solving as long as the mind is free to change, adapt, and accommodate challenges that occur constantly in the environment. As an illustration, when individuals first learn how to solve problems in mathematics, considerable focus on the specific process is required, which in this case is a particular formula. As soon as the formula is mastered, the task becomes automatic and habitual. The mind is free to attend to other matters of interest. However, in relation to this issue about the use of mathematical formulas, one can seek other alternatives to solving these problems. This resonates well in the school system, in relation to the problem of closing the achievement gap among students of different backgrounds and experiences. If the attitude to teaching and learning is liberated to meet the challenges of a changing school environment, the achievement gap between all students might be closed. Then the idea of equal education for all students will be accomplished.

Furthermore, Dewey (1930) also emphasizes the idea that some habits, like social customs, can become "ruts" that limit and constrict human behavior and achievement, especially when humans encounter something innovative. For example, those encounters can include the unforeseen challenges of social life that are inevitable to the human experience; such as, students entering school the first time (kindergarten), teachers tend to assume students are familiar with "English language" or "school culture". Thus, Dewey (1930) declares that the main problem with the educational system is that it constantly exposes children to a "premature mechanization of impulsive activities" (p. 96). In this particular process, the habit-forming function of school limits the developing, innovative potential of the child rather than expanding it. Dewey (1930) maintains that instead of worrying about old, undesirable habits, one needs to think of some action or process that creates an entirely new habit that will produce the desired end.

However, in relation to these habits of the mind, Greene tends to believe that individuals will assume the right frame of mind that would allow them to become critical thinkers, reflective learners, and effective practitioners, if left alone. Greene argues that it is the duty of teachers to increase the imagination of the students that they teach by encouraging them to read, look, and make interpretations about what they see. Greene's theory can be accepted to a certain extent yet rejected in many other aspects regarding learning. The idea that individuals can assume the right frame of mind and become critical thinkers or commendable citizens without any guardians such as teachers is farfetched. However, there seem to be a double standard in her argument concerning the process through which humans acquire habits of the mind. In one instance, Greene clearly identifies the duties of teachers, and in another work, she completely rejects the needs of teachers. However, there is one implication that Greene fails to analyze in her work. She fails to incorporate the external influences that affect learning, especially when she disregards the role of teachers. One of the disadvantages to Greene's theory is that the external influences of society will have a stronger effect if there are no teachers. Either way, Greene's argument fails to account for the role of the media and various relationship developed by individuals as they go through life, a process which Dewey called experience.

Moreover, Greene's (1965) theory of community seems to focus on the use of imagination. Greene claims that imagination should be used to apply to concepts about all things. The use of imagination fits into many encounters in everyday life, and one can agree with Greene that social paralysis can be cured by constantly re-activating the imagination. This use of imagination to start and end processes is more evident in the educational sector. For example, in kindergarten and elementary school, students are taught to use imagination; unfortunately as students get older, no one seems to evoke or discuss the use of imagination. Does this mean that the abandonment of imagination in elementary schools leads to what Greene refers to as "social paralysis" later in a student's adult life? Greene's theory of imagination is convincing in that it allows individuals to see things from different perspectives, allowing individuals to overcome what has been taken for granted and allowing individuals to expand their knowledge gained from experience. An example is a teacher in a classroom who is working with a student who has difficulties in learning. Imagination, instead of the norm, will allow the teacher to see a different method of approach in order to support the student. The imagination theory by Greene seems to account for everything that individuals take for granted. With imagination, the rich will help improve the lives of the poor; individuals in the center (between the poor and the rich) can imagine lives outside the realm of the rich or the poor, and the strong will imagine the weak. Could we imagine how teachers, educators, parents, and members of the community could close or even eradicate the achievement gap among students of various cultures if they could use an ounce of imagination when interacting with a school aged child of a different race or gender or who comes from poverty?

Michael Apple (2000) argues that, in a community such as the school environment, people may concurrently hold "progressive" and "retrogressive" positions on social issues. Michael Apple use the following examples to describe and strengthen his argument,

> Some women teachers may be very conservatives in class politics, supporting policy that can extend the expansion of powerful economic influences in all our lives. However, at the same time, these same teachers-as women-may actively work against sexist policies and curricula that harm their female students. Or, if the teacher is an African-American woman, she may be an activist in the struggle against racism, but may believe that many feminist issues are largely those of White, middle-class women. (Apple, 1993, p. 7)

These "progressive" and "retrogressive" attitudes of people in society, especially among the poor and the marginalized, account for many problems that exist in our school system today. Could this indecision also account for the current disparities in our educational system? When a Latino American or an African American student is asked to speak properly or take responsibility for his or her actions, in an instance, this request relates to his or her culture, and it is acceptable. However, if it is not something close to the culture, yet the proper thing to do for humanity, it seems unacceptable.

Influence of Theorists on Education Today

Because he contributed many innovative ideas to the field of education, Dewey might be considered among the first educational philosophers. Dewey intended to move education from an individualistic perspective to a communal view and to envision a new education in the light of larger changes in society. Dewy sought to observe changes that occur in society and reflect those changes within the framework of the educational system. Dewey seems to agree with the idea that changes in the community should also drive changes in education. Dewey was as concerned with societal development as he was with education. For example, Dewey would probably consider the changes in technology today, such as the use of computers and cell phones, as important as what students are learning in school, and because he believed that education should be as much like experience as possible, Dewey might want education to reflect these changes, especially in the new technologies.

Dewey's ideas about education certainly seem to be very prophetic today. Many years ago he wrote that "knowledge is no longer an immobile solid; it has been liquefied. It is actively moving in all the currents of society itself" (Dewey, 1915, p.25), a response seen repeated in Thomas Friedman's (2005) book, *The World is Flat*. Present-day educational technologists often suggest that educators are still operating with an industrial model of education, but Dewey, who lived during a time when the Industrial Revolution was exciting and new, mocked the same system as archaic. Dewey criticized school systems as "made for listening" with "enforced quiet and acquiescence" and "silence as a prime virtue" (Dewey, 1915, p. 22). As a result, Dewey felt that schools had only modest space for the child to work. They were instead designed to handle students "en masse" and did not provide individualized instruction. Dewey argued that knowledge gained in schools was not used in life, and he asked a question that is still relevant today for our society: "How many came to associate the learning process with ennui or boredom?" (Dewey, 1915, p. 24). Ultimately, Dewey considered school a shallow means of knowledge transmission, and he felt that the danger of school becoming irrelevant "was never greater than at the present time, on account of the rapid growth in the last few centuries of knowledge and technical modes of skill" (Dewey, 1916, p. 9). Little did Dewey know that this trend would continue exponentially in the twenty-first century and that the contrast between school and students' after-school lives would continue to grow. An old school system that requires students to be the passive recipients of knowledge cannot compete with the active learning that takes place in today's new technologies. Thus, Dewey's educational theories were the bridge between changes in the society, such as improved technologies and how students are taught in classrooms to meet the demand for the new technologies that are here to stay.

Furthermore, Dewey (1915) imagined an "individual mind as a function of social life – as not capable of operating or developing by itself, but as requiring continual stimulus from social agencies, and finding its nutrition in social supplies" (Dewey, 1915, p. 23). Dewey also believed that social forces were responsible for the development of the mind. In keeping with Dewey's belief that students have learned a great deal from their environment before beginning school, it might be said that changes in individual households, especially concerning income and family values, are responsible for the development of students' minds long before they reach the school system today. Thus, Dewey would have agreed that a change in the socio-economic status of individuals is one of the major reasons for the achievement gap among students in the school system today.

Adler was one of the first educational theorists to call for the same quality of education for all children with no exception. Though his emphasis was on the "how" to produce competent citizens in a democratic society by formal education, did what he wrote over a century ago about education and systems of reforms have anything to do with the achievement gap that exists today between African American and Latino American students and their European American counterparts? Was that what Adler had in mind, or was he making an indirect reference to the social injustice that had infected the educational process in the United States? In the beginning of his book *The Schooling of People*, Adler notes,

> A democratic society must provide equal educational opportunity not only by giving to all its children the same quality of public education-the same number of years in school-but also by making sure to give all of them, all with no exceptions, the same quality of education (Adler, 1902, p.4).

Adler seems to believe that the system of education in the United States does not provide a quality education or an equal education for all of its citizens. In relation to the discrimination and segregation that existed in society and educational institutions when his book was written, Adler never mentioned what groups in society he was addressing. Adler's argument about education was mostly targeted to the poor European Americans who actually shared the same dilemma with minorities, such as African Americans, Latino Americans and other immigrants. Nonetheless, his theories of reform in reference to today's achievement gap in education between minorities and the majority was true for all citizens and was the beginning of a change toward an inclusive educational system in the United States of America.

Adler was also one of the first educational theorists to expose the hypocrisy in the educational system in the United States. The mixed message in American society was and still is visible, but it seems that anybody who discussed this hypocrisy ended up marginalized or was considered an unpatriotic citizen by many. Part of the educational hypocrisy that Adler referred to had to do with the promise of a democracy for any nation. That promise means that a nation guarantees an equal education for all its citizens. If the United States is the most powerful democracy that exists, an equal and quality education should be provided for all its citizens. Adler leveled a particularly unflattering accusation at schools and our society when he stated that:

> We must end that hypocrisy in our national life. We cannot say out one side of our mouth that we are for democracy and all its free institutions including, preeminently, political and civil liberty for all; and out of the other side of our mouth, say that only some of the children-fewer than half-are educable for full citizenship and a full human life (Adler, 1902, p.7).

Adler's theory of education seems relevant; because his theory points out that the achievement gap in public school today is a result of human policies towards educating the future adults of our society. Adler's ideas demonstrate the disparities that still exist today in fulfilling the schooling so promised by the process of democracy. In one instance, Adler mentioned how students are divided into different groups, those that are privileged to get educated and those who are left behind. In this regard, it seems that Adler was also making reference to special education programs that have also financially plagued schools without results. Schools could do a better job than isolating these students and claiming that they are not educable. As Adler noted, "With the exception of a few suffering from irremediable brain damage, every child is educable up to his or her capacity" (Adler, 1902, p.7). What Adler is saying here is that one type of educational system is not viable for all children. Since we all come from different households with different beliefs, Adler is right. Educating a person should be a process tailored to the individual's needs. The mentality of one-size-fits all needs to be adjusted to meet the needs of all students. This is very much visible with students who have been marginalized by economic status and lack of family cohesiveness. Adler notes that there is no such thing as non-educable students; rather, we have students who have received an unequal upbringing in comparison with others. Considering the present-day achievement gap among students of different cultures, Adler seems to agree that there is no such thing as un-teachable students, only students whose parents, communities, and teachers did not prepare adequately.

Adler also discusses how formal schooling does not prepare students for further learning. Adler calls for further schooling or extending the years that one has spent in acquiring the skills that creates and makes him or her educated person. Adler's theory of education is right. The simple fact that an individual has completed some process in education makes him or her competent to join the work force. Adler calls for more training beyond the school framework of the curriculum that determines what formal education is all about. A good example of what Adler proposes is very practical in the teaching profession. There is no amount of education that could prepare a teacher of any grade for the act of teaching. This is most visible act in Pk-12 education. Many teachers regardless of academic work need to actual go through the process of learning how to teach by working as a student teacher or through on-the-job training that involves placing a new college graduate in a classroom as a substitute teacher before assigning them to a formal classroom. This training must be done in order for teachers to actually call themselves professional teachers. This process is what Adler called "internship", which should be the training that leads to a complete and acceptable education for all citizens of America.

Like Adler, Greene believes that by looking at the present situations of both schools and communities in American society, individuals need to seek alternative way of living in order to break the habit of the same routine day-after-day and to look for opportunities. Greene argues that to find these opportunities is to discover possibilities in everything. Greene (1965) refers to these possibilities as "new ways of achieving

24

freedom in the world" (p. 14). In other words, Greene's educational theory is focused on solving social problems using the values and norms that hold a community together, instead of quick fixes.

Greene also acknowledges that freedom in relation to what one does is the product of a good education. If education is the product of one's freedom, then seeking and acquiring education for all citizens of a community should be a number one priority. This allows civil society to thrive and progress without chaos. However, freedom as a product of education does not fit into what is being observed in many Pk-12 classrooms. It seems like the freedom established in the United States years ago by the founding fathers have been taken for granted. Greene notes that being free is most profound when accompanied by a good education, but many classrooms of today lack the urgency to create or develop minds that will think freely and exercise this freedom. In other words, the achievement gap between students of different cultures can be due to a lack of responsibility on the part of teachers, students, and parents. According to Greene, there is always an excuse for what affects the academic performance of certain groups of students, and these excuses have led to many accommodations in the classroom, which Greene argues is the easy way out. Greene also argues that apart from encounters in the changing world, there are other factors, such as the effects of the environment, class status, economic status, physical limitations (disability), and personal opinions that also interfere with our lives, including the achievement gap between students of different cultures.

Greene's educational theory is very convincing in several ways. First, it is a practical ideology and accessible to all who wish to improve their lives. Secondly, this theory seems to take into account all the circumstances that affect an average person, such as environmental conditions, social status, economic status, and disabilities. Thirdly, Greene's educational theory provides a working knowledge of school improvement if reform is sought to accommodate all students. Finally, Greene's theory calls for individual improvement; that is to say, the responsibility for educational advancement is the sole duty of the individual who seeks knowledge and freedom.

Greene's educational theory is relevant, but fails to account for the human nature of people that make up the community. Yes, freedom through education can subdue chaotic behavior in a civil society but it cannot negate the culture that is experienced in different homes. These cultures, according to John Dewey (1916), are the experiences that the student brings to the school. How can these different cultures from different homes benefit individuals and their community? According to Greene, educators, including teachers and parents, need to use their imaginations, to consider the child's background, and then with gradually introduce and assimilate the child into the new culture.

Greene is right; with this system in place, the achievement gap between students of different cultures will be narrowed, if not completely eliminated.

Similar to the other theorists, Apple believes that there are differential powers in education. He notes that

> The large-scale social forces such as racism and sexism many of us rightful condemn are not abstractions. Their effects are visceral. They are not far removed from daily practices, but constitute, and are constitute, by them (Apple, 1993, p. 2).

Apple's educational theory is right. In relation to racism and sexism, it looks good when in public to deny social injustice, but in private, it is justified. This social injustice of racism and sexism seem "subtle" yet not "so subtle". According to Apple, the conservative wing of a political party in the United States drives the agenda about social injustice. Apple notes that social injustices such as racism and sexism involve the "politics of our knowledge" in the educational community. The idea that institutions of learning, especially Pk-12 institutions, are aware of the differences that exist among students, yet refuse to adjust in order to accommodate these differences is a problem in itself. This ignorance of the existence of differences among people in a community, especially in the schools, has led to the legitimatization of racism and sexism in the daily

27

lives of most people. Racism, sexism and all other social injustices do not fit into our educational agenda or goals. However, Apple believes that the conservative right wing of the government propagates these injustices. Institutions left on their own, without policies and mandates from the government, could be managed effectively. The reason is that when a government assumes power (be it conservative or liberal), it usually has different agendas and policies to improve schools. It might be right to say that schools should find ways to operate without the stronghold of government policies and mandates. For example, the current movement of establishing charter schools has led educators and the community to assume an effective role in managing a school. Regardless of their problems, charter schools have stayed on course, reducing social injustices that have plagued public schools over the years. In addition, charter schools have also narrowed, if not closed, the achievement gaps that exist among students of different cultures and abilities (Hoxby and Rockoff, 2004).

Apple (1993) notes that despite the "highly publicized failures of the state bureaucratic socialism", individuals should be mindful of what the state "economic" and "cultural system does" (p. 4). The culture of a community is based on how much wealth a person can accumulate and the success in producing that wealth. According to Apple, this idea leads to a rejection of those individuals who cannot produce wealth or contribute to society. This, Apple agrees, does not only exist in the general community, but is also very common in schools. The inequality that fills our schools is the result of the quest for economic prosperity. The notion that everybody is different in the ability to accumulate wealth does not mean that one group should be treated differently from another, especially in our schools which are charged with creating equality through a proper education. This will also lead to an understanding of the historical analysis that in turn led to differences in economic status, which created inequalities in wealth accumulation. Methka et al. (2006) compared the present economic situation in America today with the game of monopoly. Methka et al. described the economic power, including accumulation of wealth that Apple (1993) seemed to emphasize, in relation to these simple concepts: To whom did the prospect of accumulating wealth favor at the beginning of the Industrial Age? According to Methka, et al., economic prosperity favored an average European American male who ran the plantation and owned slaves, banks, and the government. It was not too long ago that women and minority groups were given a chance to participate in the electoral system; and the United States then claimed that they were a free and equal system of government. Thus, by the time minorities could catch up in accumulating wealth and enjoying the economic prosperity of the nation, all available resources has been accumulated and possessed. The result of this is that minority groups maintain the same status year after year.

A good example of this is in the housing industry. Through the process of capitalist ideology, minority groups that started late could not compete effectively; therefore, renting from those who have accumulated lands and houses from generation to generation is the only option. This idea about economic disparities has also led to the achievement gap between minority students and their majority counterparts (Aaron 2007).

Apple's educational theory is convincing because economic and academic disparity is very visible in our school systems. These disparities might be subtle compared to many years ago, but they are still present in today's society. This is especially evident in the rapid decline in academic performance in many public schools across the country (Peebles-Wilkins, 2005). On the other hand, Apple's educational theory fails to account for governmental changes that occur as a result of the electoral process. Each government party in power has a different agenda and different policies for our national educational system. Hence, there is a need to create uniformity or non-partisan government for policies that govern our school systems. This non-partisan effort could be realized if educators, including teachers and parents, play active role in driving the policies that shape the educational system of each school district.

The Concept of Freedom

Dewey referred to freedom as the ability of individuals to look at their goals and desires and to change them as they see fit without outside interference. His thoughts here are similar to the thoughts of Apple and Greene. These three theorists (Dewey, Apple and Greene) seem to leave the ability to be free to the individuals not the society or institution. These theorists also believe that the changes brought about by individuals helps communities grow; this is what Dewey called experience. Dewey, Apple, and Greene possess different thoughts about freedom from Adler. Adler defined freedom as the rights and duties accorded to individuals in a just society. A just society is a society where everybody is treated equally and where the government automatically transfers the rights and freedom to the people in the community. Adler's ideas seem to focus on the government responsibilities to its citizens. In this case, Adler believes that the government should control and carter for the well being of people and this creates a fair society. Adler's thoughts here are different from Dewey, Greene and Apple. Adler tends to leave the freedom issue to society instead of to individuals. In other words, Adler believes in an organized system in a community. Apple also believes in the removal of organized institutions from the everyday life of the society. His thoughts here are similar to Dewey and Greene's thoughts. Dewey, Greene, and Apple seem to leave freedom to the individual, not to society or the institution.

Individual Freedom and Society

Dewey believes the relationship between individual freedom and society is about having a choice and being able to exercise that choice in a society. Dewey's ideas are similar to Adler's ideas and Greene's ideas in that they believe in organized institutions but with rights and duties given to individuals. Apple does not prescribe to this thought. He wants an unorganized setting for individuals. Individual freedom is the right and duty that creates a just society. Adler's ideas are similar to Dewey and Greene's ideas in that both believe in organized institutions but with rights and duties given to individuals. Apple does not prescribe to this thought. Apple wants an unorganized setting for individuals in a society. Again, Apple is not specific in addressing the issues of rights and freedom in society. However, Apple seems to imply that individual freedom is plausible if society create unorganized institutions. He is different from Dewey, Greene, and Adler because he does not believe in organized institutions. Apple argues that an organized institution has a tendency to create a class system. Apple believes that the class system created by organized institutions also creates economic disparity, segregation, and inequality in the community. One can agree with Apple's theory since this is also visible in the schools in terms of an achievement gap between minority students and their majority counterparts. Apple's educational theory does not use words such as "minority and majority". He believes that those words among others are some of the words that an organized institution uses to create inequality in a society.

Contributions to Education

According to Dewey, education needs to prepare individuals to understand their service to society, to develop self-direction, and to contribute to the community. This is similar to Greene and Adler's thoughts in that they prescribe to individual duty to society. Dewey, Greene, and Adler differ from Apple because Apple does not emphasize individual duty. According to Alder, freedom is the right of individuals in addition with the duty they exercise in a society. Education in itself plays a significant role in teaching students about their rights and their duties. This is similar to Dewey's thoughts, in that Dewey prescribes to the individual's duty to society. Dewey's ideas are also different from Apple's ideas because of the lack of concern for individual duty as expressed by Apple. Apple differs from Dewey and Alder in that Apple believes that individuals should be able to do as they please, with no sense of duty to society.

Education and Culture

Dewey wanted education to be not only theoretical in nature, but to also give individuals the opportunity to use their judgment to change their communities, if needed. This idea is similar to Adler's ideas about education. Adler believed that allowing individuals to use their judgment to change their community aspire some kind of organized system within the community and education. This will give individual's right to be part of the organized education community. Adler's ideas are completely different from Apple's ideas because Apple believes that we should completely abolish education and allow individuals to acquire knowledge through experience alone. Adler asserts that education should be developed through curricula that are the same for all students, with moral and intellectual disciplines that could set individuals free by harvesting their power to judge freely and to exercise their free will. This idea is similar to Greene and Dewey's ideas about education. Adler's ideas about education are completely different from Apple's ideas about education because Apple believes that we should completely abolish education and allow individuals to acquire knowledge through experience alone. Apple's theory about education seems to focus on the "de-schooling" of education, separating learning from social control and matching individuals who share the same issues or principals that are socially, intellectually, and emotionally important. Apple's ideas are radical in that he focused on the agenda of the government or the political party in power to determine if the policies set by that body fit the needs of all citizens. Most of the time, Apple tends to disagree with the conservative left wing ideology about education, stating that their policies favor only a few groups in society. If Apple was in charge, government would have no part in developing policies for our educational systems.

In light of the work of Dewey, Adler, Greene and Apple, it is evident that the learning environment can be affected by the economic status of individuals, the community, and the government and that learning can be socially negotiated. Educational reform generated from the community, from individuals, and from the government is also the vehicle for affecting positive social change. Clearly, changes and improvements in the economic status of a group of people will be a powerful tool in closing the achievement gap between minority students and their majority counterpart.

Each theorist sees education as an integral part of life. These theorists are interested in education and democracy. Dewey (1915) agrees that a progressive school would focus on "living primarily, and learning through and in relation to this living" (p.28). To accomplish this, Dewey believes that schools will offer access to "all the media necessary to further the growth of the child" (p. 55). Today, with the rise in the achievement gap between minority students and majority students, the media that Dewey discussed should focus on the economic status of each school-age child and his or her family. If Dewey were alive today, he would probably let nothing stand in the way of providing economic assistance to non-performing students and their families. Dewey has always argued that the most important thing to reform in education "was not the question of the waste of money or the waste of things...but the primary waste was the waste of human life of the children while they are at school, and afterward because of inadequate and perverted preparation "(Dewey, 1915, p.35).

Adler, Greene, and Apple share these sentiments from Dewey. In keeping with Dewey's love of democracy, Adler proposed a reform that would extend the number of years required for completion of a formal education. During his lifetime, Adler became the leader of **The Paideia Proposal**, which created an educational manifesto that is still visible in our present-day school systems across the nation. Greene added to Dewey's ideas about education by including the use of imagination and self-renewal through the thoughts and freedom of individuals. Apple shared the struggles that still exist when one political party creates an agenda and policies that infringe on the rights of the poor and oppressed who are not successful in an educational environment. In summary, these theorists would probably have agreed that the achievement gap between minority students and their majority counterpart should be the number one priority for educators and policymakers to address in the current educational system.

Section II

LEARNING COMMUNITY AND
ACHIEVEMENT GAP

The change in demographics of the student body, which has occurred in education over the years, has overwhelmed the public school system (Spady, 2001). Public schools of today face unique challenges in being culturally responsive and providing quality education to culturally diverse and low-income family. The academic achievement gap related to low-income and affluent groups and to African American and Hispanic American students and European American students poses the need for new and innovative interventions by educational institutions. School administrators, teachers, counselors, parents, and community leaders are in a unique position to assume responsibilities in reducing academic disparities among all students.

These sections of the book will describe the findings in existing literature about achievement gap between African American, Latino American, and European American students. More specifically, this section will examine the literature related to the characteristics of learning communities that influence the achievement gap as well as administrators' perceptions of the achievement gap in public schools. The sections will also review the literature that describes how public school teachers and administrators can close the achievement gap and how family socio-economic status is related to the achievement gap. The summary will analyze the gaps and deficiencies that were found in the literature related to the achievement gap in public schools.

Closing the Achievement Gap

Biologists claim that human beings are the slowest creatures among living things to evolve physically. Can one correlate the evolution of human beings to how the American school system evolves? Just as slow as human beings evolve, the American school system is progressing just as slow. In the eyes of many 21st century educators and researchers in the field of education and members of the business communities, the present system of education is not serving the needs of all citizens, at least those that call United States home. The traditional system of education that worked for students before the landmark Supreme Court decision, *Brown vs the Board of Education* which was passed in 1954, is not viable in today's society. There is still subtle and pervasive discrimination visible in the American school system (Vang, 2006; Wilson, 2006; Alson, 2006; DeCastro-Ambrosetti and Cho, 2005; Bol and Berry, 2005). The demographics of the student population have changed significantly; yet the system, style, and processes of schooling still remain the same. This change in the diversity of the student body in public schools has created a cultural clash between teachers, students, and parents (Mink and Duke, 2006). In responding to this change in the student body, Washor and

Mojkwoski (2006) suggest changes that need to be made in the educational system to accommodate those individuals who have been marginalized, so that a quality education can be provided for all students. In the following subsections, the literature that discusses what teachers and administrators should be doing to close the achievement gap will be investigated. The purpose this section is to review the literature about the various ways that teachers and school administrators could help to close the achievement gap between African American and Latino American students and European American students.

There is a constant public outcry toward teachers, administrators and educators to change how they are educating future American citizens. Educators need to innovate and accommodate the needs of all students and close the achievement gap between African American students and their European American counterparts (Peebles-Wilkins, 2005). Lee (2004) and Washor and Mojkowski (2006) noted that a prominent idea in closing this gap is to use personalized instruction, which allows students to learn at different rates and styles. In personalized instruction, teachers and educators need to break down lessons into common tasks but not set unattainable time frames to accomplish each task. Second, all students need to work at a pace and style suitable for them. The tasks presented to students should come from familiar resources, from either personal experience or the experience created by the teacher, as part of the knowledge required to complete each task. This type of instruction will force classroom teachers to move away from the traditional system or the idea of the "one-size-fits-all" mentality. For example, some high schools in Africa emulate the European style of education. In their system, special education does not exist; there are no services for identifying the gifted student. This European system acknowledges that if a student does not perform to a certain standard, the student is tracked into a type of vocational program. In actuality, this process worked somehow; students were leaving high school knowing what to do, despite the horrific state of the national economy. In contrast, in the United States, many high school students leave high school without any idea about what to do. The only option besides a low income job is to attend college, for which they are poorly prepared (Wilson, 2006). The irony is that the majority of these students attend college using student loans from banks, which they cannot pay back due to the fact that they did not complete a college education. Therefore, teachers, administrators, and educators should change the style of their instructional delivery in order to close the achievement gap between students. Personalized instruction is one of the processes that could close this achievement gap among all students; not only does this achievement gap affect students of school age, but it manifests itself during the adult lives of these students.

This idea of personalizing education for

each individual is consistent with William Spady's outcome based education. According to Spady (2000), three goals drive this new approach to creating curricula. First, all students can learn and succeed, but not on the same day or in the same way. For example, students learning Isaac Newton's three laws of motion should not be expected to master the law and its applications in the real world during one class period or even a few classroom periods. Second, each success by a student breeds more success. As the students learn each of the three laws of motion and master its real world applications, they are motivated to proceed to the next law. Third, teachers control the conditions of success. Teachers should praise, celebrate, and acknowledge publicly each successful milestone for each student. In other words, students are seen as totally malleable creatures. If the right environment is created, any student can be prepared for an academic or vocational career. Spady (2000) argues that one of the solutions to close or even narrow the achievement gap between African American students and European American students is to custom fit the school to each student's learning style and abilities. It is very important to mention, at this juncture, that these approaches work for all students, despite their race, ethnicity, gender, or socioeconomic status.

English Language Learner (ELL) students are another group that contributes to achievement gap that public schools have not addressed effectively. According to Vang (2006), school administrators, teachers, and policy makers should pay attention to the needs of African American students, especially ELL students, and they should plan effective instructional strategies in literacy that will produce success for all students. For example, most teachers believe that all children entering kindergarten come with certain prior knowledge of what school is supposed to be. Within this adopted school culture, the majority of teachers and administrators refuse to accept the fact that certain students enter school with limited knowledge in literacy. In fact, it is children who have been exposed to books or have been read to by their parents who are the ones that actually come with some type of literacy background that is expected by teachers. These expectations are what Vang (2006) calls "the hidden agenda in the school system" (p. 4). According to Vang, this agenda is hidden because these expectations are not clearly presented for all to see, but are used to further marginalize students who are not prepared for school in the first place. Garcia and Guerra (2004) concur that when a student violates teachers expectations of the hidden curriculum, cultural clashes can lead to "retarded" thinking. This is the type of thinking on the part of the teacher that leads to the blame game, in which students and families are blamed for the student's academic failure instead of the learning environment. Thus, if teacher expectations of students' pre-literacy abilities are not satisfied, these teachers could develop low expectations of these students, which usually lead to teacher-designed instruction that fails to meet the needs of the student. However, Ming and Dukes (2006) suggest that the problem is not that the student does not bring a wealth of knowledge to the classroom, but that the knowledge they bring is quite different from what the teacher expects. In order to understand this problem, teachers should be aware of this situation and add to the wealth of knowledge that the student brings into the classroom. If not, teachers and administrators run the risk of developing low expectations for these students, which might lead to academic failure. In support of Ming and Duke, Lotan (2005) proposes that teachers prepare lessons based on a student's previous academic performance, achievement, skills, and intellectual diversity already present in their academic knowledge.

Lotan (2005) proposes that teachers need to understand Gardner's theory of multiple intelligences and how this theory plays out in relation to culture, diversity and the teaching and learning that take place within the confines of a classroom. Lotan argues the need for teachers to encourage the use of classroom abilities familiar to students and to address the common issues that affect student performance. For example, in preparing a lesson in the science topic of gravity to a group of students, the teacher must sort out prior knowledge first before presenting the information. In this case, to activate previous knowledge and enhance understanding of this subject, the teacher should utilize examples about gravity from sports such as basketball soccer, football, or hockey, depending on the demography of students in the class. If a teacher has a group of African American students in class, to activate past experience and wake up interest, it is reasonable that references to a basketball game or football might be used to teach the concept of gravity. Many African American students are familiar with a basketball game or even any sports-related terminology. Nonetheless, the teacher must also find other examples not familiar to students and create a bridge in order to show how both references are connected. This process of linking familiar and non-familiar references is also important for many African American students because it encourages the creation of appropriate cultures in the schools. In addition, visual representation in the form of field trips or videos and DVDs will increase the probability of improving student comprehension, retention, and interest in the subject matter. These inferences work well for science and mathematics education since these subjects are the areas where the achievement gap among African American, Latino American, and European American students is the widest, according to Bol and Berry (2005).

Another area to which teachers need to pay special attention in order to close achievement gap is the use of firsthand knowledge during teaching and learning. According to Taylor (2005), firsthand knowledge is referred to as any information, knowledge, and ideas passed along from one person to another by show, touch, and tell and which utilizes the majority of the sense organs. Secondhand knowledge involves no showing and only telling with limited use of the sense organs. Taylor (2005) argues that when knowledge is passed from one person to another by mere conversation, parts of that knowledge may be lost or misrepresented due to the individual's perceptions and interpretations. For instance, a teacher can use firsthand knowledge and teach students about the different types of plant leaves and can physically bring different types of leaves into the classroom; this can be compared to a teacher teaching the same concept without the physical presence of this material. Students who see and interact with different types of leaves will learn and comprehend more compared to students who just hear facts about the different types of leaves without the actual experience of seeing and touching them. In this regard, teachers need to prepare lessons to create an experience and performance rather than just telling students and creating passive bodies in a learning environment. This style of presentation can reach all students and improve achievement regardless of ethnicity, gender, or socio-economic status and keep students focused throughout the class period.

These methods are only a few of the methods that are used in many classrooms. For instance, Gary Phillips, director of the Butler Leadership Center School Improvement Project at Butler University in Indianapolis, Indiana, points out that there are 63 known teaching methods that are commonly used in classrooms (2002). Phillips also encourages teachers and educators to add or invent their own favorite methods of teaching to the list. Out of these 63 methods of teaching, Phillips argues that many of these methods are not useful when it comes to teaching diverse group of students, especially students who have being marginalized by ethnicity, gender, and socioeconomic status. According to Phillips, the following are the most common methods of learning in schools and the least effective as measured by enduring effect, an effect that its benefits last longer: lecture or learning by listening to experts; testing as teaching; classroom seatwork which involves learning from supervised study like doing the questions at the end of the chapter, and audio visual learning from listening to the radio, audio tapes, or through instructional films or slides. In addition, some of these methods are often used for expediency rather than for the efficacy of the methods, and teachers may use some of these methods as a time filler when otherwise unprepared. The one method that was found to improve achievement was learning by teaching others or tutoring (Phillips, 2002). This is one of the most effective and enduring methods according to Phillips. Research done Phillips has shown that 90% of the retention of learning is correlated to the learner teaching others. If this is the case, then teachers in the classroom are actually teaching themselves, not students. Hence, teachers need to be aware of this method and develop strategies to reverse the process of learning from teacher to student. Another method that enhances student comprehension and improves achievement scores is cooperative learning or learning by participating in groups who assist each other and compete with other groups rather than individually. This cooperative learning method is effective if teachers use the concept of an athletic team as applied to new learning. In this case, students are teaching others and learning as teachers (Phillips, 2002).

Teachers and administrators seek different ways to improve teaching and learning and to help their students achieve subject mastery. Bloom (2000) developed the mastery learning method, which is learning through a formal, planned process of accommodating learner uniqueness and adjusting time and methods appropriately. In mastery learning, students of all background will move at a pace and time suitable to them. In a recent study (Lotan, 2006), this method demonstrated that 95% of students will attain mastery of content. Many educators seem to favor this method. According to Lotan (2006), mastery learning is also the best method for students who are struggling academically. The only downside is that this method takes much time for preparation and requires careful planning and patience from the teacher.

The other method that the literature presents as a possible solution to the achievement gap is self-directed learning. This is a learning method accomplished by designing and directing one's own learning. Gibbons (2000) acknowledges that 80% of all students' learning is a result of self-initiated efforts, rather than formal schooling. In order for this argument to hold, students need to learn to be resilient and become active learners, instead of passive learners, in the classroom. While this may be true, should teachers teach resilience as well as their content material? Some educators may be in favor of teaching resilience, and others may oppose the idea. However, many educators strongly believe that in order to close the achievement gap among African Americans and, Latino Americans and European American students, all instructional methods that improve academic excellence for these students should be utilized. Thus, teaching resilience should be part of teachers' daily tools to improve teaching and learning for African American students and other disadvantaged students.

In this section, the literature about what teachers and administrators should be doing to close the achievement gap among all students was reviewed. According to the literature review, there are also many types of teaching methods that teachers need to employ in their schema to close this achievement gap between African American, Hispanic American and European American students. The best methods should be used at the discretion of the teacher and should depend on the diversity of students present in the classroom (Lee, 2004). The more diverse the classrooms, the more methods for instruction need to be used to equalize the playing field.

48

Again, this is an area that each teacher needs to approach with prudence.

Administrator Perceptions about the Achievement Gap

Considering American educational history, one could say that administrators must have extensive qualifications to direct or guide the current educational system. According to the United States Department of Labor statistics (2008), educational administrators are responsible for constructing educational requirements, goals, and visions; they are also responsible for mapping out the best route to achieve them through the use of educational policies and procedures. Their position in the educational system requires them to take on many roles. Administrators act as managers and supervisors and support staff, teachers, counselors, librarians, coaches, and other school employees. In addition, educational administrators assume many tasks and responsibilities. They develop academic programs, monitor educational progress for students, train and motivate teachers and other staff, manage career counseling and other student services, administer record keeping, and prepare budgets. Administrators also develop relations with parents, prospective and current students, employers, and the community. In smaller organizations, one administrator may handle all these functions. In large school systems, responsibilities are divided among many administrators and support staff, each with a specific function.

Nonetheless, the responsibility of educating all students equitably and establishing the normal functions of school are the primary tasks of a school administrator. In many cases, school administrators carry out these tasks effectively, only if they wear a second hat, which involves the role of navigating the intrinsic complexity of politics (Alson, 2006). According to Alson, racial politics makes it even harder to discuss those issues that create an achievement gap between African American and Hispanic American students and European American students. For example, as a school administrator, Alson shared his experience involving closing the achievement gap. Alson claimed that closing the achievement gap drew criticisms from various groups that were directly involved in the situation. One group of African American and Latino American parents, whose children performed above standard, protested that their children were unjustly marginalized in the schools. These parents presumed that none, including the media, talks about the success of High Performing African American or Latino American students. Another group was the European American teachers. Alson (2006) argued that these teachers found it difficult to face the facts about the achievement gap between African American and Latino American students and European American students because these teachers felt that they could be labeled as racist. Thus, racial politics makes it difficult for the principal to carry out his or her administrative duties effectively.

Although the responsibilities of school administrators are well defined for most school systems, these responsibilities have no significant impact on student's general achievement score. A longitudinal study conducted by Chamber, Hylen and Schreiber (2006) affirms that the administrator's role in schools does not affect student achievement. However, Chamber et al. believe that the more parent and peer support a student receives, the higher their achievement score. In another study, Taylor (2005) stated that the high turnover of school personnel, the more school mandates, policies and procedures emerges. Taylor argues that change in leadership could also affect how school policies and procedure are implemented. A constant change in leadership without transitional processes in place will further marginalize students who are at risk. As a remedy, Taylor (2005) recommends that religious and community leaders play an active role during major personnel changes and transitions, such as the departure of a school principal or a district superintendent. However, the idea of allowing religious leaders to play an active role in the leadership of public schools could be challenged. There is no doubt that religious leaders may make some positive contributions to closing the achievement gap; however, their presence in public schools would defeat the democratic principles by which the common schools were founded in 1837 (Greene,

2007). In addition, the presence of religious leaders in public schools will create another dimension to the already sensitive decision-making processes of the Principal-ship.

Principals are the educational administrators who manage elementary, middle, and secondary schools. They set the academic tone and actively work with teachers to develop and maintain high curriculum standards, develop mission statements, and set performance goals and objectives. Principals confer with staff to advise, explain, or answer procedural questions. They hire, evaluate, and help improve the skills of teachers and other staff. They visit classrooms, observe teaching methods, review instructional objectives, and examine learning material (Ming and Dukes, 2006).

Principals also meet and interact with other administrators, students, parents, and representatives of community organizations. Over the past few years, decision-making authority has increasingly shifted from school district central offices to individual schools. For example, the number of charter schools and schools that use site based management schools has increased in many school districts. With this shift, school principals must meet the needs of all students, parents, and the faculty, including the teacher's union. School principals have greater flexibility in setting school policies and goals, but when making administrative decisions, they must pay attention to the concerns of parents, teachers, and other members of the community. This is important due to the fact that principal's role might affect how the parents and community work with the principal. Many schools have developed an organization called the School Improvement Team (SIT) that helps the school principal share decision-making responsibilities. This team is usually comprised of students, teachers, parents, community members, and administrators. Another organization found within the realm of school management is the Parent Teacher Organization (PTO). Unlike the SIT, parents of the students run the PTO; teachers and administrators are encouraged to attend meetings but generally do not run the organization. Although schools have developed this process of family and community involvement, many educators are not satisfied with the level of parental involvement in school decision-making (Chambers, et al., 2006). On the other hand, Farkas, Johnson, and Duffer (1999) claim that, even though parents strongly indicate their willingness to be part of school management, they do not know how to proceed. Doyle and Doyle (2003) surmised that schools that create communities empower parents in the process of educating their child, if allowed to be equal partner in the decision-making. School administrators should work harder in supporting parental involvement in school leadership. As one approach, schools need to create a parental leadership plan for each school year and provide a detailed account about how schools should share authority with parents and the community through the Parent Teacher Organization or the School Improvement Team. Working effectively with the school principal, these groups would ease the workload of the administrator and establish democratic governance for the school.

Preparing budgets and reports on various subjects, including finances and attendance and overseeing the requisition and allocation of supplies are important responsibilities of principals. As school budgets become tighter, many principals have become more involved in public relations and fundraising to secure financial support for their schools from local businesses and the community. Principals must take an active role to ensure that students meet national, state, and local academic standards. In relation to this role, Spady (2001) supports school reform efforts that are based on changes in the economy and technology, as also noted by Cetron and Cetron (2004). Spady argues that these changes in the economy will force school administrators to find creative strategies to serve the learning needs of all students academically and financially. These changes in our society also strongly affect the principal's perceptions about the achievement gap and the morale of the school as a community. If a school is well financed, then the school administrator can focus on teaching and learning. On the other hand, if a school is under- funded, the principal spends more time seeking funding for the school.

Many principals develop partnerships with local businesses and school-to-work transition programs for students who are challenged socially and academically. Increasingly, principals must be sensitive to the needs of the rising number of non-English speaking students and to a culturally diverse student body. In some areas, as Cetron and Cetron (2004) point out, growing enrollments also are a cause for concern because they lead to overcrowding at many schools. When addressing problems of inadequate resources, administrators serve as advocates for the building of new schools or the repair of existing ones. During the summer months, principals are responsible for planning for the upcoming year, overseeing summer school and programs, participating in workshops for teachers and administrators, supervising building repairs and improvements, and working to ensure that the school has adequate staff for the school year.

Schools continue to be involved with students' emotional welfare as well as their academic achievement. As a result, principals face responsibilities outside the academic realm. For example, many schools have enrolled growing numbers of students from dual-income and single parent families or students who are themselves teenage parents. To support these students and their families, some schools have established before school and after school childcare programs or family resource centers, which may offer parenting classes and social service referrals (Peebles-Wilkins, 2005). With the help of community organizations, some principals have established programs to combat increases in crime, drug and alcohol abuse, and sexually transmitted diseases among students, which have being identified as some of the major issues that affect the achievement gap between African American, Hispanic American, and their European American counterparts. Peebles-Wilkins (2005) acknowledges that issues of low academic performances are challenges to school administrators, but this seem to be an area of expertise for social workers. Thus, Peebles-Wilkins encourages some type of collaboration between school principals and social workers in all areas of students' academic life, not only their social and emotional needs.

The literature points out that more research is needed to examine the perceptions of school administrators in relation to the achievement gap between African American and Latino American students and European American students in public schools. Hence, one has to use caution in generalizing administrators' perceptions of this achievement gap for all schools nationwide or even for all urban schools. Each district school board may want to consider conducting survey research to determine whether administrators in their districts have differing perceptions of their schools' achievement gap. By understanding each other's perceptions, administrators and school board members will be in a better position to work together to best serve their students and narrow or perhaps close the achievement gap. Helping students to make contact with adults who have specialized teaching areas and skills can be exciting for young people. But there is also a need for students to experience relationships with adults in which they feel known and supported. These relationships should be the key to creating responsible learning communities.

Characteristics of Learning Communities

When it comes to discussion of the achievement gap, schools tend to focus on the immediate academic needs of students rather than the future. Taylor (2005) argues that students who succeed academically are most likely become successful citizens as adults. For example, should schools keep their focus on test scores as one of the major means of improving student achievement? Alternatively, should schools concentrate their efforts on applied learning that gives students immediate employment hope? Either way, consideration of these two questions may help narrow or close the achievement gap. In the following section, the literature will be reviewed that explores the characteristics of a learning community that needs to exist in order to assist close the achievement gap.

There seem to be three influential factors that transform a person from a child to a responsible, successful, and contributing adult in society; those three factors are family, organized religion, and school. Each of these three areas of the society needs stability and consistence in order to positively impact the lives of students and the community. The familial environment is deteriorating: others, instead of immediate family members, are charged to raise school-age children. This has an enormous effect on the psychological development of school-age children. In addition, grandparents often do not have the energy required to raise school-age children. Participating in an organized religion is no longer a priority. Only a few people attend church, and the few who actually attend church are often senior citizens. The absence of organized religion in the lives of school age children seems to affect the moral standards of most of these students, as they get older. The same absence of religion also creates a lack of community cohesiveness that exists in other communities that embrace some type of religion. Thus, the only area that seems to play a significant role in these students' lives is the school community. If the above is true, schools should revamp the way they carry out business to meet the needs of present-day students. For example, many students come to school every day without breakfast; however, schools serve lunch to students. Public schools should establish a breakfast mandate, allocating time to serve breakfast to all students before class begins, regardless of economic status. I learnt recently, many schools are serving breakfast to students before class. Having an empty stomach can deter a student from participating in his or her academic work (Vang, 2006). Lunch for some students tends to take place around the middle of the day, leaving many students with an empty stomach for more than four hours. These students can lose energy because of lack of nutrients, hindering the attention span needed to focus on learning. These breakfast and lunch requirements for schools need to be open to all students, not only students of low-income families (Alson, 2006). Schools cannot monitor or dictate the behavior, attitudes, and responsibilities of parents with their children at home; however, schools could do the right thing, filling those areas in which parents are deficient. Those areas include breakfast, oral and physical hygiene, and dental and medical checkups. After all, students spend majority of their productive time at school (Ming and Dukes, 2006).

Public schools need to graduate from the old system of using testing as the major part of evaluating student learning and seek other ways of evaluating students. One of the possible solutions to this problem is a performance-based educational system. In this system, students at the middle school level or who are entering high schools are asked to complete different tasks in different content areas for each year in high school (Rhode Island Department of Education, 2007). For example, a ninth grader would complete his or her regular classes, take final exams, and create a portfolio that demonstrates the work he or she has successfully completed in that school year. This student would also complete comprehensive course assessments (CCA). For these assessments, each teacher would choose three themes as the focus. The themes would be illustrated or depicted through an on-demand task, a performance task, and an extended task (Rhode Island Department of Education, 2007). In the on-demand task, students would be given one class period to complete a certain task. For the performance task, students would be given two to four class periods to complete this task but the task must be completed in the classroom. For the extended task, students could have two or three weeks to complete this task, either in the classroom or at home. Each of these comprehensive course assessments should be graded and returned to the students. Students who are not proficient in any of these assessments are given the chance to redo their tasks until they are proficient.

These different assessments from different content area teachers should be specific in their evaluations. Examples of specific evaluations could measure levels of critical thinking skills, technology skills, and communication skills. Every teacher in each grade, starting from grade 9, should have these three evaluations in mind when designing the CCA. The schools need to agree on school-wide rubrics for grading the criteria of these skills in critical thinking, technology, and communication. If possible, teachers who teach the same content area could swap students papers or projects for an evaluation. This exchange would provide further objectivity needed to observe student performance. Following these assessments, schools should also include final exams in various subjects as part of these end-of-the-year assessments. However, this final examination should only be a fraction of the total grade required for a student to exit a class or to graduate. This final exam should not be a major part of an evaluation, since many students do not perform well in testing. If performance-based assessments are carried out from grade 9 to grade 12, one could discover that the students have accomplished quite a lot as opposed to the traditional system of education that involves testing that is scheduled infrequently. These traditional examinations have no significant role in students' lives when they enter the job market of today's economy (Taylor, 2005; Scales et. al, 2006; Lotan, 2006; Wilson, 2006; Washor & Majkowski, 2006; Ming & Dukes, 2006). However, the new system can allow teachers to focus on the skills in critical thinking, technology, and communication that students need to be effective in the real-world job market. Moreover, because teachers and students will have several opportunities to re-visit these academic themes in every grade starting with grade 9; these themes will continue to be reinforced. For instance, if Johnny was struggling with critical thinking skills in grade 9, he will have the opportunity to re-visit these skills in grades 10, 11, and 12 before graduation. Hopefully, Johnny will master critical thinking skills before graduating from high school. This performance-based style of education is similar to what Wilson (2006) emphasizes in her essay. Wilson described the skills that need to be included in the educational system in order to close the achievement gap; hopefully, those skills can also close the economic gap. However, teacher unions and school administrators will need to work together to improve teaching and learning. The gap in communication and accountability among school personnel, students, parents and the community has regressed. This lack of communication between teachers, administrators, and parents has led to a blame game in which the school blames parents for a lack of cohesive communication, and the parents do likewise (Ramirez, 2000; DeCastro-Ambrosetti, & Cho, 2005). Who should be held accountable for the achievement gap? Does the school community need to create a strategy of accountability to resolve this achievement gap?

To establish a measure of accountability, everyone who has anything to do with educating a child should be held accountable for that child's education. The way to create this accountability and possibly close the achievement gap is for the school community to create strategies to encourage and monitor student academic progress. First, schools should develop a written contract involving the institution, students, and their parents. This contract could be given any name, but it should have the school mission statement. This contract should have a section for a student pledge and signature; a section for parents' pledge and signature; and a section for academic teachers' pledges and signatures. Second, schools should encourage parents to be aware of their children's grades. If schools were to send quarterly progress reports of all students' academic work to parents, then schools could encourage parents to review these reports and set up discussion meetings with various teachers about their children's progress. Third, at certain grade levels, the school community should have in place a process to check the literacy and numeracy skills of students. For example, grade 9 students could be monitored for grade level performance in reading, writing, and mathematics. If any of these grade 9 students are performing one or two grade levels below their grade, they should be placed in a remedial academic program to make up for the deficiency. These students could be enrolled in the after-school programs for literacy and numeracy skills or in other programs that will help erase these deficiencies.

Other characteristics of the school community that will narrow the achievement gap include strong leadership that focuses on academic effects, positive expectations by all teachers for all students, and an orderly and controlled school environment. School leaders, such as the principal, are charged with managing the building and the academic success of all students. It takes a well-qualified and tolerant person with talents to be able to navigate students' academic work as well as managing the day-to-day operations that take place in the school. There is a big advantage in dividing the responsibilities of managing the physical plant of the school and the teaching and learning responsibilities of the school. In some schools, a curriculum director is appointed who is responsible for monitoring and supervising the academic work of the students. The principal then manages the teachers and the physical plant of the school, and the assistant principal manages the discipline of the students. A small school building will actually leave the all responsibilities of the school to one person, the principal. This is only common in most head start or elementary schools. Teachers' positive attitudes towards students should also be part of their professional development and training. It is not that teachers are not aware of their attitudes towards students, but there should be a constant reminder about the need for positive attitudes toward students that is provided through professional development activities. Teachers should also pay attention to students' emotional needs and provide appropriate assistance. In other word, teachers should know the demographics and the cultural background of the students in their classes.

Schools should create a learning community that not only creates prospects for higher education, but also gives students the type of training in academic learning that leads to scholarship and college admission (Allen, 2006). This will involve changing the present curricula to accommodate skills and development opportunities that motivate young adults and prepare them for success in high-growth career fields. For example, high schools need to include some type of career training for students in grades 11 and 12. This training program can be composed of technical skills such as interactive media and installing and maintaining a network system. After all, these technologies are already present in classrooms and the school community. These styles of education could interest students, increase motivation and attitudes towards school, change the traditional system of education, and ultimately increase student's achievement.

All of these characteristics affirm the idea that the school community need not only meet the heart of academic instructions, but also needs to meet the temperament of the school environment in which this academic work is being carried out. The social processes of school shape the meaning of school for both educators and students alike. These social processes can make school have an appealing atmosphere for all students and make a prolific work place for the faculty, or they can hamper them. The achievement gap between African American and Latino American and European American students is everybody's business. When communities and various stakeholders create a safe environment that educates all citizens effectively and purposefully, a security for the future is provided that all people can count on.

Socio-economic Status of the Family

Doing away with or narrowing achievement gap requires a combination of school improvements with reforms to narrow the vast socioeconomic inequalities in the United States (Spady, 2001; Peebles-Wilkins, 2005). Recognizing the effects of socioeconomic disparities on student learning is not "making excuses" for poor instruction or "letting schools off the hook" for raising student achievement (Scaley-Ruiz, 2005; Taylor, 2005; Allen, 2006; Chambers et al, 2006; Dearing et al, 2006; Ming & Duke, 2006; Scales et al, 2006; Wilson, 2006). Although teachers are well aware that all students have the ability to learn, they also know that poor health or less secure homes can hinder the learning process among students. Refusing to acknowledge these issues prevents educators from properly diagnosing educational failure where it exists. Different social and economic reforms, such as ensuring good pediatric care for all students, instilling good nutrition, expanding existing low-income housing subsidy programs to reduce low-income family's mobility, supplementing the income of poor working families through the Federal Earned Income Tax Credit (EITC), and funding after-school programs could have an obvious impact on student achievement. In this sub-section, the literature related to the effects of a family's socioeconomic status as it relates to academic achievement will be scrutinized.

When analyzing parental socioeconomic situations and the role it plays in the achievement gap, there are many influential variables to consider, such as human capital, family structure, neighborhoods, socioeconomic resources, household resources, and material hardship (Ducan & Magnuson, 2005; Scaly-Ruiz, 2005; Chambers et al, 2006). However, many researchers in the social sciences have concluded that socioeconomic status in itself is irrelevant to the achievement gap. Rather, it is the psychological impact associated with socioeconomic status that actually affects the children who are reared in families of poverty. Thus, the focus of the achievement gap should be on students' well being, which includes not only their parental economic status but also the emotional status of the children. The major areas of parents' socioeconomic status that have connection with children's well being are income, education attainment, family structure and beliefs, and neighborhood conditions.

Family Income

The household income of a family is part of the social issues that affect the achievement of school-age students. Although familial participation is an important factor in child development, there is another factor that significantly affects a child's learning, and that factor is family income. Usually, an affluent family has access to many resources that give children a big edge in academic achievement as opposed to a non-affluent family. As a typical example, financial resources can enable affluent parents to secure access to good nutrition and health care, a good learning environment apart from the school, a safe neighborhood, and good educational institutions, including colleges and universities. Considering these factors, there is enough evidence to explain the large disparities in the achievement gap between poor families and rich families. A study by Duncan and Magnuson (2005) indicated that a disparity in the achievement gap exists between the very poor and the very rich; however, this gap does not exist between middle-income and high-income families. Duncan and Magnuson (2005) suggest that increasing the household income of families with young children can help poor children more than the wealthier families. Smith, Brooks-Gunn, and Klebanov's (1997) study suggested that reform of the welfare system affected children's development positively because low-income families are able to make enough money that they can provide such things as good health and nutrition that are important in the children's development. One strategy that needs to be included in solving the achievement gap is to encourage low-income parents to participate in the job market and reduce their dependency on government assistantship, in the form of a welfare check. Another strategy is to increase the amount of income of poor working families through the federal government earned income tax credit. According to Duncan and Magnuson (2005), the large supplement from the government, the earned income tax credit, in 1997 moved about 2.2 million children above the poverty line. Duncan and Magnuson also argue that providing income support for low-wage workers, such as the tax credit, encourages parents to work when they might otherwise depend on assistance from the government. This type of governmental assistance can help parents to allocate more time to raising their children as opposed to working long hours. This assistance does not only provide nurturing for the child, but also helps students with their academic work, such as completing homework that could have been forgotten without parental supervision. This behavior of completing assignments and turning them in on time can assist in closing the achievement gap.

Human Capital

Human capital includes parental skills that are acquired through formal or informal training and that are important for maintaining a high paying job and maintaining an orderly home environment (Duncan and Magnuson, 2005; peebles-Wilkins, 2005). Attending and graduating from school is the most visible form of human capital. Duncan and Magnuson (2005) have shown that higher education leads to better employment and a larger income for a family. Duncan and Magnuson also argue that the more educated parents are, the more capable they will be to help their children navigate the educational system, and including helping their child with homework and advocating for the child's educational and psychological needs. This parental assistance is very important for students in middle school and high school. Parents who are deficit in these areas need to be an active member of the school improvement team (SIT) or the parent-teacher organization (PTO) and other groups formed by school system to meet the needs of a student. Through these groups, parents can initiate a process that can assist those students who lack human capital. One can strongly argue that if parents were not successful in school, there could be resentment and mistrust of the school system, and these parents may actually guide a young child unsuccessfully in his or her academic endeavors. Again, this is the areas where parents are encouraged to get involved in all areas of the school system that serve the children, regardless of their educational attainment.

The work of many more researchers (Duncan and Magnuson, 2005; Alson, 2006;Wilson, 2006; Vang, 2006) on educational attainment have suggested that improving the educational level for mothers who did not finish high school has a high probability of improving their children's academic achievement. An intervention worth noting is to encourage the PTO or SIT to promote educational activities among mothers and their child. Good examples are programs that encourage teen mothers to complete school after the birth of a child. Another alternative is to have the government social programs provide monetary benefits to parents who complete their formal education. Since there is no law about how to raise a child, understanding the roles and behaviors of parents in a child's life during formal education could provide insights in closing the achievement gap among all students.

Family and Neighborhood Structure

Although many school-age children are born out of wedlock, eventually quite a few of these children will end up living in single parent home at some point of their childhood (Muktha et al, 2005; Duncan and Magnuson, 2005; Wilson, 2006; Dearing et al, 2006). This finding becomes a problem for children because of the financial burden that exists in single family homes. According to Duncan and Magnuson (2005), children in a single family home experience poverty that is much more profound compared to an intact family. Also, the decline in income after divorce has striking and lasting psychological effects on children. First, financial constraints may push single parents to acquire a second or even a third job in order to supplement their income. In doing so, the single parent has lessened valuable time needed to raise, discipline, and help or support their children, which can hinder their development. Sustaining the family financially can eventually result in a lack of supervision and support, which takes away a stimulating and nurturing environment for the child. Secondly, many of these single-family homes tend to lack male role models, which is an integral part of the child's social development. The absence of a male role model in a family can hinder the social behavior of the child at school.

Family structure and cohesiveness is an integral part of a child's development. Nevertheless, although financial status affects child development, the family formation is another strong factor that can affect learning. For instance, children from broken families are often in worse situations academically than those students from intact families. In addition, children of teen mothers are far worse than children born of older and more stable mothers (Carlson and Corcoran, 2002). Carlson and Corcoran (2002) also argue that parental characteristics, such as educational attainment, rather than family structure or maternal age, account for the achievement gap in school-age students. If this is true, then there are several guidelines that educational institutions need to put in place to meet the needs of all students. After all, students spend a majority of their day in school rather than at home. For example, schools should have programs that target prevention of teen pregnancy by reducing sexual activity; if possible, schools should encourage the use of contraceptives. As another prevention method, schools can implement intensive interventions that can provide mentoring and constructive after-school activities. For example, at Times Squared Academy in Providence, Rhode Island, there is an after school program called "Bridge to Success," which involves a strong mentoring program that informs young women about how they should behave. This program teaches these young women how to handle issues relating to relationships, including sex education. One can extrapolate the benefit of this type of program for public schools in terms of helping Parents Bridge the gap about lack of parenting skills. However, educational entities need to be aware of the enormous emotional and psychological needs of teenagers, especially if they are products of broken and despondent families.

Neighborhood is another factor that can shape adolescence in multiple ways. A run-down neighborhood can create problematic situations that are most visible in urban communities. Violence, gangs, drug activity, and old housing with lead poisoning problems lace these neighborhoods. Since the revenue from property taxes supports and sustains educational funding, most of these vacant and run-down properties in urban areas do not generate enough income to sustain some of the school district initiatives and programs (Ming and Dukes, 2006). Community violence, social disorganization, lack of positive role models, lack of shared values, lack of strong school and police protection, and negative peer influences can create significant stress and lead to behavior problem among school-age students. This stress can lead to a lack of academic achievement, which also leads to the achievement gap between students in poor communities and their affluent counterparts. The state and federal government should intervene in improving schools in poor communities by providing level funding for all public schools. The process of level funding has the state government filling in the financial gap that exits in urban areas by offering better funding based on needs compared to other communities that can generate funds through their property taxes alone. Schools in poor neighborhoods, on the other hand, need to create situations that encourage good parental practices, stronger connections between families and their children's schools, and a solid connection among the parents of their children's friends. As a good example, the school's PTO could organize neighborhood picnics for the children as well as movie nights, international food nights, or sporting events. These types of programs jointly organized by parents and the schools will reduce stress, create neighborhood ownership, and boost neighborhood morale. This change in attitudes and behavior can help close the achievement gap.

There is no doubt that African American and Hispanic American children are heavily affected by differences in socioeconomic status, which eventually feeds into problems related to the achievement gap. In addition, the role of genetics should not be overlooked in considering problems related to the achievement gap. However, studies have shown that there is no national government policy that addresses the issue of socioeconomic status directly. However, a review of the literature has revealed that there are several issues related to socioeconomic status, such as parental education, family structure, and neighborhood structure that need to be considered in closing the achievement gap. For example, establishing a program that could increase the educational attainment of African American and Hispanic American mothers should be considered because this initiative could significantly close the achievement gap.

Nevertheless, programs that improve the educational attainment of African American and Hispanic American mothers, increase the family income, and improve neighborhoods are valuable programs in addressing a student's environment, but these solutions do not seem to be able to totally fix what affects school-age children in academic performance (Tyson, et. al, 2005). It is worth noting that programs that focus on children's mental and physical health needs may be the most efficient way to address the achievement gap (Peebles-Wilkins, 2005). Throughout this literature review study, much has been said about the role of mothers in improving the achievement gap. However, little was mentioned about the role of fathers in this regard. What role does a father play in the educational attainment of their child? The role that fathers play calls for further research.

APPLICATION I

PROFESSIONAL PRACTICE IN STRATEGIC SOCIETAL DEVELOPMENT

The beginning of this section, section I utilized in-depth ideas from the works of Dewey, Greene, Adler, and Apple and presented a working theory of education; with emphasis on reform that could accommodate those who are marginalized. The work of these theorists characterized a learning community, such as public schools; as one that facilitates society development, democracy, driven inquiry, and socially negotiated learning. Such an environment is also a vehicle for carrying out positive social change (Dewey, 1916).

In order to provide educators with guidance for closing or narrowing the achievement gap between all students of different backgrounds, this working theory has served as a foundation for this application section of the paper. Section II was a serious examination of current issues in closing the achievement gap (between all students) in light of the working theory developed in section I. The assessment focused on the work of Washor and Mojkowski (2006) from the "Big Picture Organization." Based on the critical examination of Washor and Mojkowski and Muktha et al. (2005), it was clear that changing the approach to schooling teaching and learning, including curriculum, might provide a learning environment that fits well with the principles of societal development subscribed to by Dewey, Adler, Greene, and Apple. Creating an environment that allows all to be equal fits the need of every individual. The active participation of the community (mostly parents and students) and teacher good perception of all students in the schools can help close the achievement gap between African American, Hispanic Americans, and European American students.

Apparently it is not difficult to help a young person to experience sense of community in a special school program. However unless the program provides for intellectual engagement, it tends to serve merely a custodial function, more suited for warehousing youth than educating them. (Posner, 2004, p. 186)

In addition, active participation in the community and teacher good perception can help effect positive change in society. For example, according to Dewey (1916), education should focus and elaborate on social issues and "enhance the student's social insight and interest, so that students will be able to contribute to and improve society" (Dewey, cited in Posner, 2004, p. 181). The paper analysis also served to inform this application section of the book. Thus, both sub-sections of section I, supported the argument that an attention to individual needs, including economic and social needs, can serve as a strong base for social learning environments, and thus as instruments for effecting positive social change in formal k-12 education.

The purpose of this application section is to prepare a 3 to 6 hour hands on professional development session for providing educators with guidance in using different strategies in teaching and learning, curriculum organization, and instruction informed by theories of social needs and development to facilitate student learning. The session was delivered face to face via a Power Point slide show with segments of presentation, facilitated discussion, and hands-on activities. This companion document includes sections describing the rationale behind the session, the justification for elements of the session design, and a conclusion explaining how the theory of the previous sections is put into to practice.

Justification

This professional development session was an effort to help teachers and other education staffs better reach and better serve a generation of students who are fundamentally different than those who came before. Muktha et al. (2005) pointed out "students in today's classroom are much more diverse than yesterday student" (p. 14). Based on literature about the era of school segregation, limited academic opportunity for the ethnic minority students and their families, and race tolerance, many students can be considered latecomers in the academic field. If this is the case, then teachers have to work to eliminate the disparities in education. To go further, this course is meant both to help teachers become aware of this achievement gap and diversity and to help them bridge the gaps. The hope is that teachers might change their teaching style, perhaps even by incorporating certain cultures, in order to address the students in their familiar style.

Design and Justification

The professional development session began with the instructor welcoming participants and introducing himself, his role as an educational consultant. After the introduction, several minutes were spent on an opening anecdote, participants' introductions, and related discussion. In an effort to connect the content of the session with the participants' lives, both professional and personal, the presenter shared an anecdote about his experiences as a student. Participants were then asked to introduce themselves, and to share (in addition to their name, classroom location, and grade or subject taught) one thing they hoped for the future of education and what role they might play in it. As each participant introduced a thought, the presenter led a discussion around any related issues relevant to the class. During this discussion, many of the theories evident in the earlier sections were introduced.

Following the opening discussion, the formal content was introduced, beginning with a review of educational development and expectation of an educator. This included a review of experience, as described in the works of John Dewey and Maxine Greene. These theories were explicitly related to educational growth and achievement based learning through a discussion of the contemporary contributions of Lotan, Scales et al., Washor and Mojowski, and Muktha et al. This review was followed by a similar overview of the new material from this section. Based on the research from the earlier portion of this paper, participants were introduced to the social theories of John Dewey, Maxine Greene, Mortimer Adler, and Michael Apple. In addition to the work of the aforementioned theorists, the work of Muktha et al. (2005) on educational equality, and the work of Washor and Mojowski (2006) of the "big picture" in Providence Rhode Island on personalizing education/instruction were addressed (The MET).

Following the overview, a more in-depth discussion of each theorist began. Participants were asked to recall and share their prior knowledge of John Dewey, and many participants were able to share a good deal. The presenter then focused on Dewey's (1938) belief that experience is education, and that education should be as much like experience as possible in order to be most effective. Following the later discussion of social change, the presenter also focused on Dewey's (1916) discussion of the role of education in a democracy. The presenter pointed out Dewey's (1915) dedication to experimenting in schools in order to discover more effective practices rather than continuing in what he considered a medieval educational system. Throughout the discussion of Dewey's theories, participants drew parallels. The discussion of Dewey transitioned well into a more in-depth discussion of Greene with a discussion suggesting that if Dewey (1938) thought education was experience, and Greene (1965) thought experience was social, then education must be a social enterprise as well.

Participants were largely unfamiliar with Apple's (1993) beliefs regarding the role of conservatives in education, so these were covered as well. However, participants were familiar with imagination and experience (Greene, 1986), so discussion focused on its relevance and application in improving students' achievement. Having covered so many elements of social theory already, the following discussion of Adler was comparatively brief. Still, participants were introduced to his theory of instruction (Adler, 1903) and the ways in which he formalized social instructional strategies. Participants were also introduced to Adler's (1996) thoughts on the process and culture of education, and to his philosophy of public education. Adler was the first of the theorists discussed who wrote about educational changes, and who understood that formal education requires longer time in school or educational process.

At this point, the presentation turned away from discussing specific theorists from the earlier sections of this paper to discussion of the theories synthesized. This section of discussion began with a brief overview of "Strategic Thinking and Acting" (Spady, 2004). Prioritizing seemed to be the key word that resonates during discussion. The presenter asked three questions:

1. What is possible?
2. What is probable?
3. What is preferable?

Following this was a discussion of the role that teachers and parents could play in motivating students. The majority of the teachers seemed to accept changes to the curriculum as one of the major changes in improving students' motivation. The area of curriculum that resonated well was the "Project

Approach" (Posner, 2004). The presenter shared the advantages and disadvantages of project approach curriculum, and asked teachers to come up with ways to utilize this approach in their various classrooms, and avoid or compensate for the disadvantage part of the curriculum. The presenter encouraged teachers to collaborate across content areas if they wished to use project approach curriculum. Though this section was cut from the written version of the paper due to time and length constraints, participants were still exposed to the framework of curriculum organization, engagement, challenge, and reward that parents and the community might bring to formal education. The main point of this portion of the presentation, though, was the discussion of using strategic planning and acting to improve students' achievement. The elements of the earlier sections of the paper including the capacity for parents and community to serve as tools for effecting positive social change in schools were discussed. Here, participants were reminded of the social change agenda of Dewey, Greene, Adler, and Apple. Discussion then moved beyond these theorists to other work that is being done in the realm of effecting social change with monitoring trends in the society.

Participants were introduced to the work of Dr. William Spady on *future-focused education.* One of Spady's (2004) works was distributed for the participants to read and share out loud. This was followed by a worksheet Strategic Thinking and Acting- How

Does Your Organization Rate? (Canole, 2006).
Time was allocated to complete the worksheet
and tallied for discussion.

All of this discussion filled approximately
90 minutes, which was followed by a 10-minute
break. Then, finally, a PowerPoint presentation
was used to discuss strategic thinking and
acting to participants. After the PowerPoint
presentation, an activity created by a group led
by Muktha Jost of North Carolina A&T State
University (2005) was introduced. Monopoly, as
the game is called, is a powerful metaphorical
explanation of problems of racism, institutional
racism, and European American privilege. The
game was played as a regular Monopoly game
would be played, but players were allowed to
enter the game at different stages. Teachers were
divided into groups of six (one observer, a
banker, and four teachers). Two teachers from
each group started the game; the other two
teachers joined the game much later (about 30
to 40 minutes), one at a time. The presenter of
this professional development was not a
participant. He walked around each group
offering assistance and clarifying questions that
teachers ask. Only the observer in each group
was instructed to view the game as a metaphor
to racial equality problems of affirmative action
and privilege (Muktha et al., 2005).

Once the game was over, teachers came
together to share their experience playing the
modified game of Monopoly. Observers of the
game were grouped together. The players were
also grouped together. Each group was given a

sticky large poster paper to respond to their experience. The observer of each group was allowed to share details using the following prepared questions:

1. Who came first? Who came last?
2. How did the enthusiasm and motivation differ among students?
3. Describe the process of accumulation of capital. Who had it? Who didn't?
4. What were some comments from the players?
5. What were spending and buying patterns in the group?

The players were able to share their experiences. The following questions were used to organize the presentations:

1. When did you start? What chance did you have to win the game?
2. How did you feel about starting first or having to start the game later?
3. How did you learn the rules of the game in comparison to others?
4. How motivated were you when you started? What happened to your motivation as the game moved on?
5. How much skill is ordinarily involved with monopoly? How much with these altered rules?

When participants came together again, listening to observer groups or the players group, there were several comments, laughter, and facial and body expressions that seemed to come from playing the Monopoly game. It seemed that the majority of the teachers who participated could visualize parallels in society and education. Players who started first commented "We have the board to our self, even before others joined we had plenty of money since we had $500 each time we complete a round; and we bought many of the properties." One of the last group members commented that, "By the time I started, they didn't have a game thing for me to call my own. I had to find a penny and start my game with it. I could not compete because I started late." The observer and the banker were asked to discuss what they observed. The observer explained how playing the game and allowing individuals to join the game at a certain point got the first players motivated. The banker explained that the game made her think about the students in her class. The general consensus was that it was difficult to play catch-up if one started anything late.

If time permitted, a final discussion session was planned. Participants were to use the think-pair-share strategy to consider possible uses for different strategies in their classrooms. Each would think about the question individually, then discuss it with a partner, and finally share it with the group. Following this, they would be invited to brainstorm lesson plans using these ideas. When the session was implemented, time limitations dictated that the presenter move ahead to the final reflection questions, in which participants were asked to reevaluate their answers to the questions posed during the introduction. Participants were then asked what their next steps might be before the session was brought to a close with a final evaluation.

In the final evaluation, 100% of the participants strongly agreed that the presenter demonstrated knowledge of the subject matter and was well prepared and organized. One hundred percent also agreed or strongly agreed that the presenter was able to stimulate interest and respond to participants needs. Several participants left enthusiastic positive comments such as "Great class! Good resources!" and "The presenter was very knowledgeable about the subject matter. Thank you for your time!!! I enjoyed the presentation!"

When asked how the session could have been improved, some participants shared constructive suggestions as well. Following are some samples: "I would love to attend an in-service that would give me information specifically for primary grades: 1 – 5;" "Many of the strategies were pretty sophisticated, like for high school and up;" "My students are mostly English learners, in fourth grade. I admittedly don't know what strategies are being used at home, so I need to do a little research there;" "I would have enjoyed more time to actually explore the strategies more, rather than learning about the theorists and those people that developed the original ideas;" "I probably won't remember the names of all the theorists, but if there were a chance to learn by going online to their websites or something that would be a little more interesting. I would enjoy more ideas to take home and research or implement."

This session may be offered again as an on-going professional development for teachers, and emphasis would be focused on the use of strategic thinking and acting in education. The feedback from participant evaluations will be valuable in the presenter's effort to improve the session for these future events.

Theory to Practice

Section one of this paper presented a synthesized working theory of societal development, with a focus on the works of Dewey, Greene, Adler, and Apple. This working theory was put into practice through this application portion of the paper. It was presented to participants and discussed with them during the first segment of the professional development session. Participants might now apply this theory to their teaching and to their own awareness, experience, and imagination in the courses they teach.

The section II of the paper was a critical examination of the achievement gap between African American, Hispanic American, and European American students in light of the working theory of societal development developed in section one. This, too, was discussed with the participants in this professional development session, and participants now have the opportunity to apply the theories of Washor and Mojowski (2006), Vang (2006), and Muktha and Jost (2005) in their own classes. Along with the section one and section two portions of this book, the application portion has also supported the argument that experience and imagination can serve as social learning tools and as instruments for effecting positive social change in formal K-12 educational systems. In keeping with the underlying social change philosophy, this application portion of the book also provided participants with a hands-on segment during which they were able to experience and reflect on the role of these theories in practice. Finally, participants were introduced to a variety of ways to apply these theories in their own classrooms, including the use of cooperative learning, multicultural education, and role-playing. Ultimately, the focus was on the potential power of experience and imagination to serve as social learning tools and as instruments of positive social change. The hope is that participants will indeed apply these theories in their own roles as educators and thus ensure that the future is indeed a better place for their students.

REFERENCES

Adler, M. J. (1982). *The Paideia Proposal.* New York, NY: Macmillan.

Alson, A., (2006). Attacking the achievement gap in a diverse urban-suburban community: A curricular case study. *Yearbook of the national society for study of education.* 105(1), 49- 77.

Apple, M. W. (2000). Official knowledge: Democratic education in a conservative age. (2nd ed.). New York, NY: Routledge.

Bol, L. & Berry, III, R.Q. (2005). Secondary mathematics teacher's perceptions of the achievement gap. *High School Journal, 88,* 32-45.

Cetron, M. J., & Cetron, K. (2004). A forecast for schools. *Educational leadership,* 61(4), 22-29.

Chambers, E., Hylen, M., & Schreiber, J. (2006). Achievement and at-risk middle school student's perspective of academic support. *Journal of Research in Character Education.* 4(1/2), 33-46.

Dearing, E., Kreider, H., Simpkins, S., & Weiss, H. (2006). Family involvement in school and low-income children's literacy: Longitudinal associations between and within families. *Journal of Educational*

Psychology, 98(4). (ERIC Document Reproduction Service No. EJ746472)

DeCastro-Ambrosetti, D., & Cho, G. (2005). Do parents value education? Teachers' perceptions of minority parents. *Multicultural education.*13(2), 44-46.

Dewey, J. (1907). *The school and society.* Chicago, IL: University of Chicago Press.

Dewey, J. (1990, 1956). *The school and society; and, the child and the curriculum.* Chicago, IL: University of Chicago Press.

Dewey, J. (1916). *Democracy and education: An I ntroduction to the philosophy of education.* New York, NY: Free Press.

Greene, M. (1988). *The dialectic of freedom.* New York, NY: Teachers College Press.

Greene, M. (1995). *Releasing the imagination: Essays on education, the arts, and social change.* San Francisco, CA: Jossey-Bass.

Johnson, D. P. (2005). *Sustaining change in schools: How to overcome differences and focus on quality.* Alexandria, VA: Association for Supervision and Curriculum Development.

Lee, J., (2004). Multiple facets of inequity in racial and ethnic achievement gaps.

Peabody journal of education. 79(2), 51-73.

Lotan, R., (2006). Teaching teachers to build equitable classrooms. *Theory and practice.* 45(1), 32-39.

Ming, K., & Dukes, C. (2006). Promising practices: Fostering cultural competence through school-based routines. Multicultural education.14(1). 42-48.

Muktha J., Edward L.W., & Mark J. (2005). When the rules are unfair, but the game isn't. *Multicultural education.* 13(1), 14-21.

Peebles-Wilkins, W. (2005). Help close the achievement gap. *Children & schools.* 27(4),195-196.

Sanders, T. (1998). *Strategic thinking and the new science: Planning in the midst of chaos, complexity, and change.* New York: The Free Press.

Scales, P.C, Roehlkepartain, E.C., Neal, M., Kielsmeier, J.C., & Benson, P.L., (2006). Reducing academic achievement gaps: The role of community service and service learning. *Journal of experimental education.* 29(1), 38-60.

Scaley-Ruiz, Y., (2005). Spoken soul: The language of black imagination and reality.

Educational forum. 70(1), 37-46.

Schlechty, P. (2005). *Creating great schools: Six critical systems at the heart of educational innovation.* San Francisco: Jossey-Bass.

Senge, P et. al. (2000). *Schools that learn.* NY: Doubleday.

Spady, W., (2001). Beyond counterfeit reforms: Forging an authentic future for all learners. Lanham, MD: Scarecrow Press.

Taylor, J., (2005). Achieving excellence in urban schools: Pitfalls, and evolving opportunities. *Negro educational review.* 56(4)259-283.

Tyson, K., Darity, Jr., & William. (2005). It's not "a black thing": Understanding the burden of acting white and other dilemmas of high achievement. *American sociological review.* 79(4), 582-605.

Vang, C. (2006). Minority parents should know more about school culture and its impact on their children's education. *Multicultural education.* 14(1), 20 (Eric document reproduction services No. EJ759642).

Washor, E., & Mojkowski, C. (2006). Creating
new steps: Innovating from the edge to the
middle. *Phi Delta Kappan, 87*, 735 – 739.
Retrieved
November 4, 2007. from
http://www.bigpicture.org/publications/
washor.htm.

Wilson, J.B., (2006). Why America's
disadvantaged communities need twenty-
first century learning. *New direction for
youth development.*110, 47-52.

SECTION III

Theories of Human Development and Education

In a possible scenario, two students enter kindergarten at the same time. Book exposure and reading has been provided to student A, whereas student B has never seen a book before. The assumption here is that the student exposed to books will fare better in school than the other student. However, this information never makes it to the teacher's desk, and therefore, the same method of instruction is provided to student B as well as all the other students. In this scenario, Egan (1997) argued that student B needs intellectual tools to match student A.

The following questions arise in relation to this scenario are linked to human cognitive development. Why are some humans born with academic gifts while others are born with cognitive deficits? In addition, how is it that the operations of the human cognitive system largely remain unknown, but these operations encode who we are and what we do? To answer these questions requires an examination and understanding of human cognitive development in four areas: (a) theoretical constructs and paradigms, (b) cognitive activities, (c) practical applications to education, and (d) current research.

This section will describe human cognitive development through an analysis of the cognitive development theory by Piaget, the recapitulation theory by Eagan, and the social learning theory by Bandura. Furthermore, this paper will describe the relationship between the theories of human cognitive development and education, allude to possible avenues for further investigations, and discuss how to reach those students with cognitive deficits effectively.

Jean Piaget

When discussing the process of acquiring knowledge by reasoning, intuition, or perception in children, Poser (2004) noted that Piaget is an authority in the area of cognitive development of children and adolescents. Piaget and Inhelder (1969) understood that children created ideas. Piaget claimed that children and adolescents were not limited to receive information and knowledge from parents or educators; rather, they actively constructed their own knowledge.

Piaget's work provides the foundation for the constructivist philosophy of learning. According to Creswell (2007), constructivism is a type of worldview in which individuals seek understanding of the world they live in. Individuals tend to develop personal meanings about their experiences, often a one-sided belief that is directed to a certain object or thing. A social constructivist believes that knowledge is constructed, and learning occurs when children create products or objects that are of interest. This paradigm is used to argue that learners are more likely to be engaged in learning when these objects are personally relevant and culturally meaningful (Hunter, 2004; Marzano, Pickering,

& Pollock, 2001). In studying the psychology of children and adolescents, Piaget identified four major stages of cognitive development: sensori-motor, preoperational, concrete operational, and formal operational. In addition, Piaget also defined the concepts of assimilation, accommodation, equilibration, and schemas. The next sub-section of this paper will describe these four major stages and key concepts that relate to the cognitive development theory that Piaget created.

Cognitive Development Theory

Piaget believed all children and adolescents (referred to as youth) pass through cognitive developmental stages in order to advance to the next level of development. In each stage, the youth demonstrate new or acquired intellectual abilities and an increasingly complex understanding of the world. One cannot omit a stage; intellectual development always follows the sequence prescribed, including maturation (Piaget & Inhelder, 1969). The ages at which children progress through the stages are common to all youth; however, they may also be different according to the environment and background of individuals. For example, in relation to the sensori-motor stage, educators and parents should try to provide a rich and stimulating environment with plenty of objects to play with. On the other hand, in the concrete operational stage, learning activities should involve problems of classification, ordering, location, and conservation using concrete objects. Piaget observed that children exhibit behaviors that are characteristic of more than one stage. That is to say, the stages overlap or that there is no clear delineation of each stage.

Sensori-motor Stage. The first stage, sensori-motor, starts when the child is born and stops at about 18 months to two years of age (Piaget & Inhelder, 1969). This stage involves the use of motor activity without the use of symbols. Knowledge is limited in this stage because it is based on physical interactions and experiences. Infants cannot predict reactions, and therefore, they must constantly experiment and learn through trial and error. Such exploration might include shaking a rattle or putting objects in the mouth. According to Piaget, as they become more mobile, an infant's ability to develop cognitively increases and early language development begins during this stage. In addition, Piaget (1975) noted that object permanence occurs between seven to nine months, demonstrating that memory is developing. In other words, infants realize that an object exists after it has left their visual field.

Preoperational Stage. The preoperational stage usually emerges during the period between toddlerhood (18-24 months) and early childhood (2-6 years), (Piaget, 1977). During this stage, children begin to use language, memory, and imagination. In the preoperational stage, children engage in make-believe and can understand and express relationships between the past and the future.

Complex concepts, such as cause and effect relationships, have not occurred at this stage. Piaget argued that intelligence is egocentric and intuitive, not logical.

Concrete Operational Stage. According to Piaget (1977), the concrete operational stage typically develops between the ages of seven and 11 years of age. Using logical and systematic manipulations of symbols demonstrates intellectual development that is related to concrete objects. Thinking becomes less egocentric with increased awareness of external events and involves concrete references.

Formal Operation Stage. The period from adolescence through adulthood is the formal operational stage. Adolescents and adults use symbols related to abstract concepts. In this stage, adolescents can think about multiple things that are liable to change suddenly and unpredictably, in systematic ways. In addition, they can formulate hypotheses and think about abstract relationships and concepts. Piaget and Inhelder (1969) believed that intellectual development is a lifelong process, but upon attaining formal operational thought, there is no need for new structures. Intellectual development in adults involves developing increasingly more complex plans through the addition of knowledge.

Although Piaget (1975) presented the four stages of cognitive development, he focused on two major principles that guide intellectual growth and biological development: adaptation and organization. In adaptation, he claimed that for individuals to survive in an environment, they must adapt to physical and mental stimuli. Assimilation and accommodation are both part of the adaptation process. Piaget's assumption was that humans possess mental structures that assimilate external events and convert them to fit their mental structures. In addition, mental structures accommodate themselves to new, unusual, and constantly changing aspects of the external environment. Piaget's second principle, organization, refers to the nature of these adaptive mental structures. He suggested that the organization of the mind is complex and integrated. The simplest level is the schema, a mental representation of performance of some physical or mental action on an object, event, or phenomenon.

Assimilation and Accommodation. Assimilation is the onerous process of placing a new object into an old schema (Piaget, 1977). For example, Jacob, who is six-years-old, asks his father to buy Subway sandwiches for dinner. The father tells him to go ask his mother. When Jacob asks his mother, she says no. She explains that dinner is ready for everybody. Jacob's father asks what his mother's response is, and Jacob replies, "Mom refused to buy dinner. Mom does not love me". Jacob does not understand why his mother said no. Jacob's father explains why his mother said no. He tells him, "Mother cannot stop making dinner and buy Subway. It means she will throw food away." The father explains how people in other places cannot find food to eat, and he uses examples of the experience the family had during a vacation in Africa. Piaget noted that in order for Jacob to make sense of what his father just told him about wasting food, he would have to assimilate the information from his father into his existing internal cognitive structures. Jacob might do this by assuming that his dad was teasing him and that the wasting of food is not true. Jacob could also infer that the rejection from his mother is real as explained by his father. In this way, Jacob finds a way to fit this external reality into his internal cognitive structures. Piaget noted that assimilation occurs when a child perceives new objects or events in terms of existing schemas or operations. Piaget also emphasized the functional quality of assimilation where children and adults tend to apply any mental structure that is available to assimilate a new event and to actively seek to use this newly acquired mental structure.

Accommodation refers to the process of changing internal mental structures to provide consistency with external reality (Piaget and Inhelder, 1969). Accommodation occurs when existing schemas or operations must be modified or new schemas created to account for a new experience (Piaget, 1977). Piaget referred to the integration of the process as assimilation or the ability to differentiate between old and new experience. Accommodation plays a vital role in assimilation, and vice versa. According to Piaget, as assimilation creates reality, structures that help maintain reality are accommodated. For example, consider again the case of Jacob discussed earlier. Jacob understands that he cannot simultaneously eat his mother's food and a Subway sandwich. Thus, if his father had pointed out that his mother is making dinner, Jacob would naturally have to alter his internal mental structures to adjust to the newly discovered external reality. This might mean that Jacob would have to believe that his mother has to make dinner as opposed to buying dinner. Consequently, Jacob can see the difference between making dinner rather than buying dinner. In this way, Jacob can accommodate his internal mental structures to his external reality.

Educational Implications

An important implication of Piaget's theory is adaptation of classroom instruction to the student's individual developmental level. The content of instruction needs to match the developmental level or stage of the student. Therefore, the teacher's primary responsibility is to facilitate learning by providing a variety of experiences. Tomlinson (2004) argued that the model of instruction known as differentiated instruction provides opportunities for students to explore and experiment within their developmental level, thereby encouraging new understandings and comprehension. Moreover, opportunities that allow students of diverse cognitive levels to work together academically often encourage challenged students to attain a more advanced level of understanding.

Another implication for instruction is the use of concrete experiences to help students learn. Research (Hunt, Wiseman, & Touzel, , 2009; Hunter, 2004; Marzano, Pickering, & Pollock, , 2001; and Tomlinson, 2004) has suggested that less than 40% of high school graduates in industrialized countries accomplish academic work successfully in accordance with established or prescribed rules of operations; thus, many people do not think formally during adulthood. This fact is significant in terms of developing instructional tools that are arranged in the order in which cognitive development occurs for students, but that may be limited in their understanding of abstract concepts. This latter statement is significant for both adolescent and adult students. Instructional strategies, such as the use of visual aids and models, provide students the opportunities to discuss social, political, and cultural issues. Educators, especially teachers, should teach broad concepts rather than facts, as well as place these learning strategies in a context meaningful and relevant to the learner (Hunter, 2004).

On the other hand, some researchers have identified shortcomings in Piaget's theory. For example, Egan (1997) argued that by describing tasks with confusing abstract terms and using overly difficult tasks, Piaget underestimated children's cognitive abilities. Egan noted that researchers have found that young children can succeed in completing simpler forms of tasks requiring the same skills. However, Piaget's theory predicts that thinking within a particular stage would be similar across tasks. For instance, Piaget argued that preschool children should perform at the pre-operational level in all cognitive tasks. Evans (1973) noted that research studies have found diversity in children's thinking across cognitive tasks. According to Piaget (1977), efforts to teach children developmentally advanced concepts would be unsuccessful, yet Egan (1997) noted that researchers have found that in some instances children often learn complex concepts with relatively brief instruction. Egan also pointed out that researchers now believe that children may be more competent than Piaget originally thought, especially in their practical knowledge.

Cognitive development is an intricate process comprised of three primary concepts affecting the development process. The primary concepts are (a) assimilation, (b) accommodation, and (c) equilibration. All three concepts are associated with the creation of schemata and their modification in order to achieve a balanced sense of understanding of the external world. According to Piaget (1977), cognitive development in children is based on four factors: biological maturation, experience with the physical environment, experience with the social environment, and equilibration. Piaget referred to equilibration as the biological drive to produce an optimal state of equilibrium between people's cognitive structures and their environment. Equilibration is an attempt to bring about a state of equilibrium between the first three factors and the reality associated with one's external environment. This state must be present for cognitive development to take place. Equilibration involves both assimilation and accommodation. During each stage of development, people conduct themselves with certain coherent internal mental structures that allow them to make sense of the world adequately. When external reality does not match with the consistent internal mental structures, which Piaget called disequilibria, equilibration occurs as an effort to bring balance between assimilation and accommodation as the person adapts to more complicated internal mental structures. Human beings continually attempt to make sense of the world around them by assimilating new information into preexisting mental schemes and accommodating thought processes as necessary. This effort to maintain a balance, symbolized by equilibration, allows for cognitive development and effective thought processes (Costa and Garmston, 2002; Hunt, Wiseman, and Touzel, 2009).

Kieran Egan, Recapitulation Theory

Language or linguistics is one of the cognitive tools that shape our understanding of the universe (Egan, 1997; Piaget, 1977). Egan argued that primitive people created myths because they provide the serenity with which to observe world phenomenon and the ability to complete ideas using proper language. Stories and events were explored by using things and objects, which made sense in the language being used. Thus, Egan noted that the development of the mind, starting at age seven, includes literacy as part of its developmental tools, although not through spontaneous developmental stages, such as those proposed by Piaget. Egan introduced binary oppositions as part of language development that is found in every culture, but he provided different interpretations for each culture. He explained that binary oppositions came about due to language usage. Egan believed that humans use binary oppositions to make sense of the world. For example, the use of male/female to represent human, as opposed to the use of a person or individual, is a type of binary opposition that creates stereotyping and gender associations in the western world and many other cultures. Moreover, Egan claimed that humans naturally imbue binary oppositions, even to the point that they can be obvious in children's thinking. He noted that children create opposites and intermediates in order to make sense of things around them. For example, Egan noted that "a child concept of temperature starts by the child establishing opposites, that is, *hot* and *cold* then middle terms like *warm* is used to create range between the *hot* and *cold*" (p.40). With the development of these types of binary oppositions by children, Egan argued that eventually adults are able to recognize things that are natural as opposed to culturally altered things.

In relation to thinking in children, Egan (1997) contended that concrete thinking seems to be the armor of articulation; however, he argued that abstract thinking is present in children for making meaning out of concrete content or realistic manipulations. Egan stated:

> In teaching and curriculum planning, then, we might still hold to the principle that our understanding moves from the known to the unknown, but we would move from the known to the unknown, but we would do well to think of the known in terms of powerful abstractions and the unknown that can be tied to them. When we begin to think of telling or teaching children something, we might sensibly begin within what set of binary abstraction it can build on (p.53).

The process of thinking is used to make sense of the world. For a child or adolescent, this point has never been a topic of debate. Egan (1997) contended that several issues, opinions, and assumption have been neglected in relation to young children's thinking abilities. For example, Piaget (1977) argued that adult thinking is of the highest developmental order while the thinking of children is considered and appraised, according to stages of development. Egan noted that many researchers in the field of psychology have accepted the notion that the thinking of young children is inferior to that of adults. Egan argued that such knowledge only recognize positive gains in cognitive ability, and at the same time ignoring the losses. Thus, Egan claimed that lack of attention to the loss of cognitive competence, which does not necessarily agree with the protocol of western intellectual development, might be detrimental to children of different cultural background.

Egan (1997) believed that children go through transformations in accommodating reality between the ages of five and ten years. He claimed that at five years of age, children tend to accept what is being said to them as long as it helps keep things exciting. On the other hand, as they mature in age, children question the reality of things around them. For example, in comparing five-year old and ten-year old children, Egan noted that a five-year-old child will not ask intricate questions about a fairy tale as long as fantasy keeps the story interesting. However, a ten-year old child will ask questions to make sense of the story.

Egan (1997) claimed that the minds of human beings work the same regardless of their background. He argued that the only differences that exist in human minds with reference to cognitive abilities are the processes, which they use to make sense of the world. Egan assumed that it is possible to make sense of a phenomenon and that cognitive activities are utilized differently due to the various intellectual tools that individuals use, instead of according to their genetic makeup. In other words, Egan believed that human minds are genetically compatible in relation to understanding while the tools used by various cultures support the differences that individuals experience in their interpretation of the world. For example, could Egan's theory explain the many conflicts that exist between different countries, religions, and political ideologies? An instance might be how the Muslim interprets the Koran in comparison to how the Christian interprets the Bible in relation to the same phenomenon. These linguistic tools as prescribed by Egan could be seen differently if they are the basis of their intellectual knowledge. Egan noted, "I am claiming that, given the phenomenon of interest to this theory, the differences we note in people's thinking are sufficiently accounted for by the differences in the intellectual tools being used" (p.174).

However, Egan (1997) also argued that in some cultures, malfunction thinking is not a function of language development and the intellectual tools used for the development of cognitive abilities. Egan insisted that in order to understand differences among people's views of the world, the intellectual tools available to them are better predictors rather than their age. He claimed that various cultures have managed to create a variety of intellectual tools. Egan pointed out that linguistics is the greatest intellectual tool to have shaped human understanding of the environment.

Egan (1997) agreed that the problem with understanding intellectual, cultural, and educational development was the absence of strong metaphors to make connections. Just like many cognitive abilities, Egan noted that metaphor is one of the intellectual tools used to make logical sense of a phenomenon. For example, Miller (1973, as cited in Egan, 1997) claimed that it was possible to understand the cardiovascular system, especially the heart, blood, and blood vessels after somebody had invented pumps to clear floodwater. Thus, the use of the word *pump* became a metaphor used to clarify the process that occurs in the cardiovascular system. To bring together Egan's theory, this example calls attention to linguistics and the metaphoric sense of developing cognitive abilities in various cultures. Most significant is that the person who uses a different language does not understand the word *pump*. Therefore, what other cognitive or intellectual tools are available to help people of different backgrounds to make sense of the working of the heart, other than teaching them the English language?

Teaching for Learning

Egan (1997) believed that teaching can be placed into three different but overlapping traditions. The three traditions, as prescribed by Egan, are the socializing, Platonic, and Rousseauian traditions. In relation to these traditions, Egan stated:

> Inherited from the socializing tradition is the sense of the teacher as an initiator and role model whose primary responsibility is to guide the students into the norms, values, skills and knowledge that will enable them to approximate the idea of adult citizenship. (p.239)

In relation to the Platonic tradition, Egan claimed that the role of teachers is to imbue subject area mastery into students. In other words, teachers are the authority and experts in some area of academic discipline, and their main job is to instruct and inspire students to achieve at the highest level. However, in the Rousseauian tradition, Egan explained that the primary responsibility of the teacher is to support individual student development. Granted, separately, none of these traditions can achieve the role of a teacher, or even collectively.

Egan reported five general and distinctive kinds of understanding that teachers could merge with the above named traditions. The five understandings he named Somatic, Mythic, Romantic, Philosophic, and Ironic. Somatic understanding refers to the tools used before language was developed. This understanding includes the process of communication before the acquisition of language by different cultures. As an individual grows from child to adulthood, they acquire language, and this somatic understanding stays with the individual as they grow base on their social structure. In mythic understanding, perceptions are introduced as opposites (for example, tall/short, or hot/cold, or boy/girl). Mythic understanding also includes comprehending the world through stories. In romantic understanding, Egan compared this stage with the need to discover examples of unmatched things, such as how fat/skinny a person can be. This understanding involves associations with the quality of heroes, limits of reality, and persistent phenomenon. Philosophic understanding deals with the discovery of principles, which underlie and limits the information found in romantic information; in this case, Egan claimed that knowledge is placed into coherent general schemes. Ironic understanding represent the mental flexibility to recognize how scantily flexible are the minds of humans and the languages they use. It involves the ability to consider a different philosophic explanation of events.

Egan (1997) suggested that in order to be alert to and knowledgeable about the different kinds of understandings, teachers must navigate back and forth within these understandings to deliver instruction effectively. For example, since there are no permanent stages of cognitive development, as Piaget suggested, teachers can use knowledge in one stage to deliver instruction in another. In this case, the first knowledge will serve as prior knowledge and as the foundation for the transfer of learning for the new material. These understandings as described by Egan are not definite developmental stages, because teachers can see or approximate which area students falls in and then adjust their instructional strategies by using any or all the traditions. Egan called this type of teaching "outward looking." Egan also emphasized that these kinds of understanding are not specific stages, but are combined levels that could be used at any age or developmental stage of students. For example, if a teacher includes humor in a lesson plan, according to Egan, the humor covers the three traditional responsibilities of a teacher. At the same time, the intellectual tool informs the mythic, romantic, philosophic, and ironic appeals. The other understanding is the somatic understanding. According to Egan, somatic is very evident from birth to two years of age and is found in small pieces throughout life. The visible difference between somatic understanding and the other understandings is that all of the understandings are grounded in the somatic; that is to say, all understandings are rooted in the body. Egan believed that human exploration of the world starts from the human mind and moves to the human body and from the body out into the world. Therefore, Egan concluded that teachers would be more effective if they do not place knowledge directly into students' minds. Rather, they must guide and inspire students to expand their minds into the knowledge. For example, in teaching genetics and the principles of inheritance, instead of discussing all that is known about inheritance, the teacher could ask students to interview family members, including distant relatives about the characteristics that are seen in each family member. This information from students could be used to determine how to provide instruction about the subject matter. The work that students generate makes it easier for them to expand their minds into the body of knowledge as prescribed by Egan.

Furthermore, people may ask what Egan (1997) theories have to do with teaching for learning, which takes place in a classroom. Today's classrooms have changed in reference to transfer of learning, retention, motivation, and rigorous academic work for the variety of students (Marzano, Pickering, and Pollock, 2001; Hunter, 2004; Hunter, 1994). According to Hunter (2004), in order to make teaching meaningful and personal to students and to learn effectively, teachers must develop strategies to deliver instruction effectively to all students. Even though Egan's levels of understanding (somatic, mythic, romantic, philosophic, and ironic) are in different developmental stages, these understandings allow for forward and backward movement in stages. In order words, a student could be in a romantic stage, but can make equal sense of things in the mythic stage, if the previous stage serves to convey the knowledge better. For example, if a teacher provides instruction about a concept that seems relatively difficult to comprehend, the idea of using previous knowledge could assist students in their learning. The teacher could use the movie "The Wizard of Oz" as metaphor because the metaphor falls under the tradition of mythic understanding. However, if the student is in a high school class, Egan categorized the student development stage as philosophic understanding. The idea of using the movie "The Wizard of Oz" to connect the instruction with scenes in the movie might make sense to the

113

majority of students in the class. This argument is based on the assumption that all students must have seen the movie and they are familiar with the scenes. On the other hand, students who are not familiar with the movie will struggle with such a teaching strategy. The movie scenes are the intellectual tools that Egan addressed in relation to the teaching and learning environment. Thus, for the teacher to make things equal, he or she could show the movie first before proceeding to deliver the instruction.

In addition, instructional strategies that use metaphor, analogy, compare and contrast, and categorization enable teachers to meet students at their level, yet they are challenging enough to also meet academic rigor (Hunter, 2004). Egan's stages of development and the back and forth process allow teachers to increase student's interest in any subject matter. The process creates an atmosphere where all students participate, are highly engaged in the learning process, and are motivated. In addition, Egan claimed that the process encourages students to independently tap into prior knowledge and make sense of new material.

Educational Implications

Egan (1997) argued that the use of mythic understanding, the use of metaphors, the use of images generated from words, and the use of story structures as intellectual tools could assist in creating user-friendly curriculum for schools. For example, history or social studies curriculum in the elementary grades could be designed and presented to students as powerful and dramatic events instead of boring, romanticized, routines based on local customs. Egan suggested that history is one of the major intellectual tools, which individuals use to make sense of the changing world. Egan also explained that history is that part of human experience that could be used to make sense of different new knowledge.

Egan (1997) claimed that humor could also be considered part of the intellectual tools that can be used to develop mythic understanding. The argument is that humor can increase student vocabulary and make understanding of language explicit and reflective. Furthermore, humor can add to the ability of students to describe things, to observe, and to experience effects in the world more accurately. The use of humor clarifies the notion that words that sound alike can assume different meaning when written down. For example, the words *son* and *sun*, or *new* and *knew* sound the same, but are spelled differently. These words also possess different meanings.

Egan (1997) insisted that the old curriculum used in schools has resulted in training a mindless group of people. He cited various witnesses who commented on this classic type of education. Egan argued that these old curriculums are not enough to educate students of today's generation. Today, schools have changed demographically, and many more people are attending school than ever before. These curricula need to change in order to accommodate this new diversity of the student body found in schools today. He commented, "The curriculum I have outlined here draws on principals derived from the distinctive kinds of understanding. It leads students by a somewhat unconventional route to what seems to me, a more abundantly educated life" (p. 209).

Albert Bandura

Bandura is one of the well-known psychologists whose work in social cognitive theory has played a significant role in the relationship between a cause and effect model, which shaped the process in which behavior psychologists view human development (Costa & Garmston, 2002). Bandura (1986) proclaimed that environmental events, personal factors, and behavior all operate as interacting determinants on events carried out by individuals. Bandura argued that human thought is a powerful machine for comprehending the environment and interacting with it. In the social cognitive theory model, Bandura argued that children imitate behavior from observing others, the environment, and the mass media. Bandura's famous experiment that exemplifies his theory was the 1961 "Bobo Doll" experiment. In the experiment, a group of children viewed a documentary film of a woman beating up a Bobo doll, while shouting aggressive demeaning words. When the children were left alone to play with the Bobo doll, the children also beat up the doll, imitating the behavior and action of the women in the documentary film. The study was very significant, because it departed from the notion that rewards directs all behavior. In the case of the "Bobo Doll" study, the children received no incentive or encouragement to beat up the doll; they just carried out the behavior they observed. Bandura called this situation, molded observation learning (p. 80). The next section of this paper will analyze Bandura's social cognitive theory and its implications for education today.

Social Cognitive Theory

In social cognitive theory, Bandura (1986) claimed that individuals are not molded by some kind of inner force or external forces automatically; rather, there are other factors, such as behavior, cognition, personal issues, and environmental events that all work together to create each other. Bandura argues that these perspectives define the individual as a person in terms of basic capabilities. This next section will discuss these basic capabilities, followed by a discussion of the educational implications of Bandura's social cognitive theory.

Symbolizing Capability. Symbolizing capability ascertains that humans use symbols for change and that fit within their environment. According to Bandura (1986), the use of symbols allows people to connect short-lived experiences into an internal locus of control that serves as a guide for further circumstances. Furthermore, through symbol, people create meaning for the experiences that they have encountered. For example, the use of symbols could convey thought in an animation of subjects. In this example, one can use animation to act out a dangerous, real-life, situation that might involve saving life (i.e. the use of a dummy for cardiopulmonary resuscitation). By manipulating the symbol, which in this case is "dummy", relevant information is gained, the problem is solved, and the consequences of an action are learned without the trial and error system that would have resulted without practice. Thus, Bandura argued that the thought process needed to follow the symbolic system and external events and vice versa.

Another way to understand the symbolic capability as explained by Bandura (1986) is to actually perform some type of work on an object and then interpret the external process into a symbolic form. For example, if an individual watched a movie describing how certain people achieved great success, Bandura believed, that individuals will construct generalizable symbols of the successful strategies, rather than schemata that simply reflect how those particular people succeeded in their particular domains. This cannot be accomplished on one's own. Bandura argued that this system helps develop cognitive skills for individuals. Furthermore, children learn mathematical concepts by symbolization. For instance, a visual representation could be children learning to solve addition and subtraction of mathematical problems through physical manipulation. Here the number symbols represent objects. Using these numbers or manipulating them to solve problems correctly on paper creates a relationship between symbolic capability and thought process in humans.

Forethought Capability. The forethought capability is the ability to think of something before it happens (Bandura, 1986). Alternatively, this term also means considering or anticipating something good or bad that is about to happen based on one's behavior (Costa and Garmston, 2002). Bandura believed that people do not necessarily react to things within their environment, but that they are trained from previous experiences. Bandura agreed that human behavior, good or bad, is done to serve some kind of purpose for an individual, and that purpose is created or established by an anticipation of the behavior and its consequences. Bandura explained this idea as follows,

> People anticipate the likely consequences of their prospective actions, they set goals for themselves, and they otherwise plan courses of action for cognized futures, for many of which established ways are not only ineffective but may also be detrimental (p. 19).

Through the process of thinking of something before it happens, people motivate themselves and guide their actions. Bandura

119

(1986) argued that reducing the impact of external or environmental factors, anticipatory tendencies could support prudence behavior. In other words, people do acquire knowledge and the cognitive skills required to think, evaluate, and formulate solutions or alternatives. In addition, Bandura believed that humans possess the capability of recognizing various consequences of different courses of action. Therefore, making a decision about a course of action that does not always use the correct reasoning may be based on a lack of evaluating information or misreading the anticipated consequence. In following this thought process, Bandura (1986) confirmed that people know what to do but chose a different route because their minds are changed by immediate and confusing circumstances or emotional factors. Thus, they choose to behave differently from the norm.

Vicarious Capability. In vicarious capability, Bandura (1986) discussed how observation of other people's behavior and its consequences could take over the learning experience. He claimed that observation of other people's behavior could produce rules for generating and monitoring behavior patterns without the observant need to create the rules initially through trial and error. The observational learning process is short and quick, reducing the need to go through a tedious process of trial and error. Bandura believed that the process of observation is vital for human development and survival. In addition, Bandura believed that a lack of learning from this observational system could create costly, even dangerous effects. For instance, one cannot teach children or adults to swim, drive a car, or fly an airplane by trial and error. This example could only take place by observational learning from adequate, but not exceptionally qualified exemplars. Thus, the less humans draw their behavioral decision from an intrinsic locus of control, the higher the chance that the observational skills will be utilized effectively (Chamorro-Premuzic, 2006).

Bandura (1986) also argued that humans are born with limited intrinsic patterns. In recognition of this deficiency, Bandura argued that humans have the need to learn. The learning process needs to be accomplished through an extended period, and individuals must master new abilities throughout the life period (Costa and Garmston, 2002). Thus, Bandura stated, human beings need to be vicarious learners. For example, if a family need to transmit its language or life style to their children, they need to model the behaviors that reflect these cultural patterns, without reinforcement of behaviors that occurs by chance or luck. Bandura agreed that modeling can help master complex skills. He insisted that things such as linguistics skills, a fictitious narrative of considerable length and complexity, with characters presented in sequence and organization of action and scenes, required assistance. Bandura assumed that this sort of knowledge could only be transmitted effectively only by social cues. Bandura tried to prove that learning by observation is absolutely necessary in order for learning to occur in humans, even if there are other ways of acquiring learning. Bandura considered learning by observation modeling the shortest way for humans to acquire knowledge. For example, a teacher of any grade level in a K-12 community could learn to be an effective teacher by observing veteran teachers who have exhibited exemplary teaching methods (Aso, 2008). Bandura strongly believed that most of the psychological theories were developed and in place long before the enormous advances in technology occurred. He suggested that the new technology such as television and movies create a powerful symbolic environment that plays a big role in human lives. Thus, psychologists need to pay attention and consider the powerful symbolization produced by the media (Marzano et al., 2001; Hunter, 2004; and Hunter, 1994).

Self Regulatory Function. Another important part of social cognitive theory is the characteristic of self-regulatory function. In this part of the theory, Bandura (1986) claimed that people in general do not carry out their intentions to satisfy the need of others. He believed that people respond to behavior based on some kind of internal processes and their interpretation of those reactions to their own actions. In other words, one only responds to behavior in an environment based on his or her interpretation of the act, which is led by self-produced influences (Costa and Garmston,

2002). Bandura noted that arranging the environmental conditions, using cognitive guides, and creating incentives for individual efforts, could accomplish the self-regulatory function. However, external influences sometimes create and support self-regulatory functions. The external influence does not necessarily remove the idea that showing self-influence somehow creates one's behavior (Hunt et al., 2009).

Self Reflective Capability. According to Bandura (1986), self-reflective capability is a significant characteristic of humans. He argued that self- reflective capability allows humans to analyze their experiences and think of their own thought processes. He contended that by reflecting on their various experiences and on what they know, people can generate an adequate knowledge of themselves and the world around them. The idea of self-reflection allows individuals to not only gain experience, but it also allows for evaluation of their experiences, for monitoring ideas, acting on them, making decisions about their thoughts from the results, and creating changes as needed. Therefore, people act on their thoughts and analyze the benefit of their thoughts when they manage events (Costa & Garmston, 2002).

Human Nature. In relation to human nature, Bandura (1986) discerned that humans possess huge potential that observational experiences can model into different forms within the biological arena. Bandura stated, "To say that humans can change and adapt to the environment by observing and changing their intrinsic characteristics is not to say they have no nature, or given guidelines" (p. 21). The capability of being molded, which is intrinsic to humans, depends on the neurophysiological process and structure that has grown and developed over time (Chamorro-Premuzic, 2006). Bandura argued that these neurophysiologic mechanisms are responsible for creating symbolization, forethought, evaluative self-regulation, reflective self-consciousness, and symbolic communication. For example, the action of the adrenal medulla of the adrenal glands is responsible for secretion of the epinephrine, a hormone responsible for fight-or-flight; the same hormone is also responsible for the sympathetic nervous system (Marieb, 2003). The fluctuations of these hormones in people can alter their course of action. In this case, the sympathetic nervous system helps create the thought process used to respond to a situation. Being molded to certain characteristics does not mean that humans were not born with certain innate behaviors; some of the behaviors appear or are present at birth; and others appear through biological development after periods of maturation (Costa and Garmston, 2002). For example, nobody has to teach infants to suck or cry, toddlers to walk, or adolescents how to engage in sexual intercourse. Bandura claimed that these innate behaviors are neural physiological attributes inherited from the product of accumulated ancestral experiences that are part of the human genetic code. This is to say that both experience and physiological factors combine to form a big part of human behavior. Thus, people's behavior contains mixtures of inborn and learned elements from observing the environment (Hunter, 1994).

Bandura developed a social learning theory to help explain problems he saw with the behaviorism model of learning proposed by the well-known psychologist Skinner. Bandura's work on social cognitive theory led him to believe that behavior was not just a reaction to environmental stimuli, but could also be learned from watching a model perform the behavior and then that behavior could be reproduced. He believed that learning could be cognitive as well. Bandura found that behaviorism alone lacked the complexities of the phenomena he studied, such as aggression in adolescents, and therefore, he decided to add a little something to the interpretation of human behavior (Costa & Garmston, 2002). Bandura argued that environment influences behavior, but behavior influences environment as well. In order words, environment and behavior together play significant role in human tendencies. Bandura identified this concept as "reciprocal determinism" (p. 22). In reciprocal determinism, Bandura explained that the world and a person's behavior cause each other, and one would not exist without the other.

Educational Implications

Bandura made a major contribution to the understanding of learning and behavior in the classroom. Unlike other behavior psychologists such as Skinner, Bandura (1986) believed that learning could take place through observations. In his social learning theory, the environmental factor is not the only method for learning. He agreed that students could learn by watching models of behavior, such as parents, teachers, and fellow students. He stated that cognitive learning could be achieved by "vicarious reinforcement" (p. 19) and by observing the behavior of others. In vicarious learning, Bandura insisted that present day technology has played an enormous role in learning. He claimed that telecommunication including television and Internet have paved the way for individuals to quickly learn through observation. Children have a tendency to imitate both good and bad behaviors from what they see on television. Bandura argued that individuals could learn the likely consequences of behavior by watching what happens to others. He did agree with other behaviorists like Skinner as to the importance of reinforcement in learning and behavior. For the purpose of education in today's society, Bandura would probably agree that all adults involved in educating adolescents need to act as models. In addition, those adult models should also create an environment that is conducive for such imitations or learning to occur (Hunter, 1994; and Marzano et al., 2001).

Bandura's (1986) work could not exist without some criticisms. For example, Bandura's work on behavior is arguably more consistent than what Bandura's theory suggested (Joseph,

1985). Bandura's behavior theory focuses a great deal on a particular set of circumstances existing in a particular place or at a particular time. Piaget (1977) also argued that the theory lacks attention to biological or hormonal processes that are innate with all humans. However, the most notable criticism is the idea that the theories of Bandura do not seem to work together. Big issues like concepts and processes, such as in observational learning and self-efficacy, have been highly researched but there is little explanation about the relationship among the concepts (Egan, 1997).

Comparison and Contrast of Theories

Piaget believed that the intellectual development of humans has specific stages, and that the stages are fixed. That is to say, once an individual attains a stage, he or she will be done with the stage. Egan (1997) disagreed with the notion of fixed developmental stage. Egan also argued that humans develop biologically. However, they do not possess the intellectual tools to express or use intelligent protocols. In addition, Egan's assumption was that humans with varied culture do not share the same intellectual tools; thus, this factor hinders how individuals express intelligence. Bandura, on the other hand, seemed to agree with Egan's theory. He believed that intelligence is preconceived; however, young people need to observe how intelligence is been used before participating in the use of it.

Piaget, Egan, and Bandura were also interested in how knowledge developed in humans. Egan's developmental theory varies from childhood to adulthood, emphasizing the impact of culture and language as a means of developing intellectual tools. Piaget's developmental theory focused on childhood development. Piaget described specific levels of developments that children needed to pass to adulthood. He claimed that each stage is permanently induced. That is to say, that once an individual completes one stage, he or she, will not go back, or use prior stage(s). Egan's theory supports Piaget's theory to some extent. Egan also believed in levels or stages of development as prescribed by Piaget, but he disagreed with the idea of individuals not going back to use the pervious stages once completed. Egan argued that as they pass through each stage, individuals could go back to pervious stages, if it assisted in making sense of new experiences. Bandura completely avoided the developmental stages, but focused on the impact of the environment and other human behaviors in society as a means of acquiring intellectual capacity.

An important education implication for all of these theories is the adaptation of classroom instruction to the student's individual cognitive development. Piaget believed that content instruction should match the developmental level of students. Therefore, the teacher's primary responsibility is to facilitate learning by providing a variety of experiences. Egan believed that the content needs instruction to match the intellectual tools acquired from pervious developmental stages. The teacher's primary responsibility is to seek prior knowledge first before presenting new knowledge. Bandura's social learning theory is different from the theories of Piaget and Egan. Bandura contended that teachers should pay attention to the types of models used during instruction. However, all theorists agreed that people continue to develop intellectual or cognitive tools to navigate the world as they experience it. However, Bandura's social cognitive theory seems to focus on human behavior in comparison to Piaget or Egan whose theories emphasize human development. Bandura's social learning theory centers on the social behavior of humans from childhood to adulthood, where socialization leads to human cognitive development. This theory seems to be consistent with Egan's recapitulation theory, specifically in relation to mythic understanding. In mythic understanding, Egan (1997) claimed that socialization of humans creates the intellectual tools needed to navigate the experiences of the world. The same theory is also consistent with Bandura's (1986) social cognitive theory. Both agreed that humans needed to interact in order to generate tools to make sense of the world.

This section has described, analyzed, and synthesized the work of three theorists in human development whose world perspectives have shed light on human cognition. Thus, human cognitive development was also analyzed in relation to philosophical, sociological, and educational paradigms. The work of these theorists and their contributions to education today were also critically reviewed. The contributions of these theorists to education today were reviewed individually, and their works were compared and contrasted. In addition, the views of each theorist about the relationship between education and cognition were examined.

The next logical step is to connect the work of these theorists to some modern day examples in order to gain a deeper understanding of the implications about cognitive development for education in the classroom today. To accomplish this, a connection will be made between the theories that were presented and some real classroom examples, and a short discussion on the possible implications of this connection for future research will be presented.

In looking at the problem from the beginning of the section, from Egan's (1997) standpoint, student B has diminished or absent intellectual tools. This diminished capacity in cognitive tools may be a direct result of a lack of exposure to literacy activities, which results in a significant delay in the language structure needed to attain educational achievement. In addition, if intellectual tools are developed through structured language, as Egan believed, then it makes sense to conclude that student B is in a primitive state in terms of cognitive development. Thus, it would be difficult for student B to catch up with the rest of the class academically, unless the teacher employed a different learning style.

Piaget (1997) argued that cognitive development in humans came about due to a complex equilibration process. Scrutinizing student B using this theory, then, the conclusion is that the endless closed circuit loop that Piaget discussed may have developed an open circuit. To be precise, the information building based on previous schemes may not have occurred for student B. This shortage will complicate refraining information and make the achievement of new information unlikely for this student.

Conversely, how do the social boundaries of cognitive development play into student B's learning deficiencies? According to Bandura (1986), social cognitive development comes about because of models available for student A in his or her environment. It may be that student B, despite his or her lack of exposure, also did not observe family members reading books; thus, reading did not initiate because of a lack of an appropriate model. This fact might also lead to diminish social and emotional behavior for student B because of the lack of cognitive development models and observations.

Therefore, it is logical to conclude that for student B, the K-12 public and private educational institutions, especially individual classrooms, create a difficult and often perplexing environment. Accepting this argument, the next step in the next section

(Section IV) component is to describe current research in relation to adolescent cognitive development, particularly in relation to social change at the high school level, as well as to analyze current research that describes the cultural influences that affect children and adolescent student's cognitive development.

SECTION IV

ACQUIRING KNOWLEDGE

Countless factors affect the cognitive development of a person from birth until adulthood, including factors such as personality, locus of control, neighborhoods, schools, and culture (Bursik & Martin, 2006; Feist, 2006; Kalyuga, 2006; Margolis, 2006; Morales & Guerra, 2006; Olina et al, 2006; Pacini-Ketchabaw, 2006; Pillow, 2006; Pratt & McLean, 2006; Staudt et al, 2006; Stoeger, 2006). Educators who wish to have a significant impact on adolescents must first understand the factors that influence a human being's cognitive, psychological, social, and moral development. Educators must also understand how individuals respond to the ecological, psychological, and social circumstances in which they exist.

The role of school systems, parents, and the community in the development of adolescents is quite clear. For example, the environment provided by parents and the community is different from that of the school. Parents might decide that children must pray before meals, while public schools regard it illegal. The school environment, guided by laws and policies, is more organized when compared to the diversity of students' cultural backgrounds. In addition, the family and neighborhood could also be affected negatively by low socioeconomic status (Kowaleski-Jones, Dunifon, & Ream, 2006). As the faces of students are different, so are the homes and their upbringings different. Aso (2008) noted in a seminar that three factors influence a person's human development: family, religion, and school. Aso argued that in order for individuals to develop full cognitive abilities, those three institutions must be strong in the child's life. However, it appears as society develops, the role of family, religion, and school often changes (Nsamenang, 2008). Lately, it seems that the school systems have absorbed the role of family and religion in the development of their students. Educators and parents need to understand that the development of students is related to their assumption of various roles in society. Consequently, teachers and parents should play a more influential role in working with adolescents in order to help them achieve proper cognitive development.

The human species has not changed at the same pace as technology. Humans must adapt to this new technological society using the same biological, psychological, and cognitive resources as the humans before them. Knowledge acquired through reasoning, intuition, or perception has grown exponentially because of technological advances in society, along with the ability to do more and to do it more quickly. In other words, humans need to adapt and thrive, given the resources and innate abilities that they have at the present time. In order to take full advantage of individual potential, humans must understand their limits and resources and how they might be instruments of positive change by understanding and encouraging individual development, needs, and possible contributions.

Students do well, despite all these obstacles that challenge cognitive development (Kalyuga, 2006). However, strong parental involvement, good schools, safe neighborhoods, and positive personality traits could improve and shape human development for adolescents. The purpose of this section IV is to describe the current research literature related to the numerous interconnected aspects of adolescent human development, including cognition, personality, locus of control, the role of the school, and cultural influences. Through an understanding of these various factors that influence human adolescent development should be an appreciation for diversity, which could lead to a better understanding of human development in general and to assist individuals reach their academic potential.

Cognitive Development

The cognitive functions of adolescents experience many changes during that phase of human development. These changes continue throughout the life cycle of individuals based on factors such as academic attainment, life experiences, social interactions, and inherited traits (Pillow, 2006). These changes are also limited to knowledge, beliefs, and intentions. What adolescents understand regarding cognitive activities may serve as a gap between children's mental states and the epistemological

135

thought of adolescents and adults. In school environments that serve as a social framework, diversity in culture, language, and ethnicity generate assumptions about other people's thoughts, guides peoples' actions, and shapes interpretation of others' actions. Therefore, student knowledge of cognition will guide the student to acquire more intellectual sophistication that can be used in improving their learning, monitoring their performance, and improving their academic achievement.

Furthermore, cognitive development is not an automatic process, it is not present at birth, and it is not picked from the environment without application of some sort. Researchers have reported that cognition, although innate, is learned (Kalyuga, 2006; McLean & Pratt, 2006; Pillow, 2006; Stoeger, 2006). Cognitive processes could not be successful without passing through various stages. Piaget (1952, 1972) argued that humans pass through various stages of cognitive development at various ages in their lives in order to attain adulthood. Stoeger (2006) claimed that children will not reach any stage of cognitive development without proper education or guidance. Organized education is well suited to improve cognitive abilities; for instance, in comparing human beings to other animals, humans are the only animals able to understand and able to do what they have learned. Bandura (1986) agreed that such knowledge might come from observation and modeling in the teaching and learning processes, as seen in school systems.

Cognitive development focuses on how children learn, retain, and process information. Kalyuga (2006) argued that it is the area of development that emphasizes the system of knowledge structures. The development of the mind entails language acquisition, mental imagery, thinking, reasoning, problem solving, and memory development. Egan (1997) called the latter cognitive tools, which children need to develop in others in order to be good contributors to society. The development of these cognitive tools is the study of how these processes develop in children and adolescents, and how they become more competent and valuable in their perception of the world and in their use of various mental processes. Pillow (2006) noted that many children less than five years old possess basic understanding of mental states, such as recognition of knowledge, ignorance, desire, emotion, and intentions. Young children do not fully understand cognitive activities such as selective attention, inference, or interpretation that would influence a person's mental state. Pillow noted that understanding many cognitive activities seems to begin between the ages of five and seven; the concept of cognition becomes more sophisticated through adolescence and adulthood. Children's thinking is not the same as adult thinking. When a child goes through developmental stages, their thinking changes; this change Pillow identified as occurrence knowledge, organizational knowledge, or organized knowledge structure, and epistemological thought. These three areas of cognitive development are not a distinct sequence of development as suggested by Piaget (1975), but similar to the developmental process proposed by Egan (1997). For instance, each developmental stage is unique; however, they could have common characteristics and inform each other. Among the three areas of cognitive development, Pillow noted that it is epistemological thoughts that appear during late childhood (between 13-14 years of age) and continue to develop through adulthood period.

Occurrence Knowledge. Recollection and forgetting are part of the occurrence of cognitive activities in children. During elementary school years, their thoughts, in comparison to older children, are undeveloped and inadequate. For instance, three and four-year-old children will not articulate, understand attention, inference, and interpretation of cognitive tasks. When compared to children five to seven years of age, these parts of cognitive tasks become articulated. In addition, children learn cognitive behaviors that include imagining stuffs that do not reflect reality (Pillow, 2006). Children's tendency to observe other people's cognitive behavior enables them to explain the same uncharacteristic events. For example, a child may ask his or her mother to pick him or her up at school early on Thursday and Friday because of teacher conferences. Yet the mother shows up at the regular dismissal time. The child's perceptual experience is that the mother should remember the changes for the two days. The child's mother not coming at the newly changed time would conflict with his or her knowledge or schema. Thus, if the child is aware of processes such as forgetting or distraction, the mother's mistake might be reasonable. Pillow claimed that the words "remember and forget" (p. 26) are difficult terms for children to comprehend. Within the context of the example above, children typically replace remembering and forgetting to mean correct and erroneous action, regardless of the person's past knowledge.

Organized Knowledge Structure. Many researchers agree that childhood brain functions are not organized as compared to that of an adult's (Pillow, 2006; Olina et al. 2006; Stoeger, 2006; Kalyuga, 2006; Johnson et al. 2006; Pancini-Ketchabaw, 2006). However, the same researchers have claimed that during middle childhood, the desire to think and reason appears to be part of the brain, making it a valuable information-processing center. At his stage of development, the constructs of reasoning, remembering, learning, and imagining contribute to the construction of beliefs. At a point in late childhood, having acquired knowledge of occurrence of cognitive abilities, Pillow noted that children start to organize knowledge as different cognitive processes. In comparing children's cognition with adult cognition, Pillow noted that children emphasize information processing more than certainty, while adults emphasize certainty more.

Kalyuga (2006) noted similar pattern of results. He presented cognitive load by creating instruction for two levels of learners in computer adaptive-based tutoring in kinematics. Similar to the previous study, the instructions reflected similar information-processing scope, and adult learners' emphasized certainty more than the children did. Stoeger (2006) claimed that as children develop an understanding of cognition, they see cognitive activities as organized, logical, and deliberate acts instead of individual occurrences of some activities. For example, children learn to complete homework activities independently without reminders or prompts, and they begin to realize that completion of such work will assist with mastering the subject.

Epistemological Knowledge. This is the third and final stage of cognitive activities following organized knowledge structures. Pillow (2006) suggested that the transition from childhood to adolescent thought is an important milestone in children's appreciation of subjectivity. He claimed that subject thoughts appear early in children but in limited capacity. However, Stoeger (2006) noted that epistemology could be supplemented by arbitrary variables that include motivation and favorable environmental circumstances; therefore, epistemic beliefs will affect learning abilities more than age. This is in agreement with Pillow's beliefs that during early childhood, knowledge of mental functioning in terms of children's belief systems is well organized. In addition, the belief system from childhood transcends to reasoning where adolescents understand the mind to be the center of information. The mind can serve as a product of children's belief system. Without the basic belief system, children could not have the tools to develop and grow cognitively. In contrast, Kalyuga (2006) emphasized the need for a system or organizational method to continue nurturing the process of cognitive developments. Kalyuga acknowledged that regardless of age or developmental stage, cognitive activities will not be effectively accomplished or sustained without cognitive-supported environments. That is to say, without a cognitive-supported environment, children might not immediately arrive at the epistemological stage of cognitive activities. In addition, the lack of a cognitive support system will hinder the potential of adolescents and many adults to maintain cognitive activities.

Natural versus Artificial Selection of Knowledge. Disposition and other factors such as height, weight, strength, and birth order that occur during developmental stages are natural selection issues that can affect cognitive development. Artificial selection, on the other hand, involves all things available in the environment to assist a child in acquiring some knowledge (Johnson et al., 2006). An example is distinguishing between a child's speaking and a student's differentiating between vowels and consonants in school. The learning in school is artificial, and the speaking is natural.

Experience versus Maturity. Cognitive development seems to rely on biological development and organized knowledge, which serves human needs better in development. Researchers agree that cognitive development favors maturity in place of experience (Kalyuga, 2006; Olina, 2006; Pillow, 2006; Stoeger, 2006). Cognitive development occurs when children mature; this process occurs naturally in humans. One interpretation is that children acquire cognitive abilities when they are physiologically ready, and therefore, there is no need to imbue a sense of cognitive development until the child is ready. Another interpretation is that children develop through regular practice of cognitive activities (Kalyuga, 2006). Other researchers agree. For example, Olina et al. (2006) argued that the more children practice cognitive activities, the better they become at navigating the world effectively.

Competence and Performance. It is challenging to observe what a child is able to comprehend and do as well as how they perform in cognitive activities in comparison to adolescents and adults. Children do poorly when tested in areas of cognition by researchers (Margolis, 2006; Meier, 2006). This finding may be in part due to various uncontrollable circumstances; for example, some children may perform a task with ease at home with parents and relatives, but the same children might not attempt anything when tested in the absence of their relatives. This underperformance may be due to an unfamiliar environment, test administrator, or test anxiety. This issue of nonperformance in testing situations regarding children's cognitive development is vital.

Personality Traits

From the dark ages to the period of enlightenment and Piaget's cognitive development theory, emphasis has been on cognition as a major part of the processes of development. Other areas such as personality traits have not received equal attention, at least not until recently. Humans in the past have accepted personality traits as a myth, an illness, and a taboo, especially if the personality trait does not conform to society norms. Research pioneers in the field of behavior psychology, such as Pavlov, Skinner, Bandura, and Watson have facilitated the understanding of personality traits as a legitimate part of psychology. These theorists have also assisted in negating the myth that certain personality traits are of a result of demonic influences (Driskell et al., 2006; Fuller & Coll, 2010; Johnson et al., 2006; Livas-Dlott et al., 2010; Torelli & Kaikati, 2009).

Researchers define personality traits as acquired and inherited characteristics observed in humans that influence cognition, motivation, and behaviors in unusual circumstances (Feist, 2006; Johnson et al., 2006; McLean & Pratt, 2006; and Premuzic-Chamorro, 2006). The work of Egan (1997) clearly identifies how humans, especially non westerners, could make a correlation between personality traits and some demonic principles. Egan proposed that this thinking was in part due to limited skills in linguistics, not to demons. He noted that multifarious unexplained physical phenomena could be identified with non-linguistic characteristics, and those that fall short of linguistic tools are, therefore, unable to be explained and not capable of communicating the idea that the phenomenon generates fear in human. Instead, demonic principles become a way to make sense of what is unimaginable. Livas-Dlott et al. (2010) also suggested that the linguistic circumstance of individuals is in part culturally specific instead of demonic. For example, Livas-Dlott et al. reported that Latino-American parents read to their children less than European American parents do. This one social activity plays a significant role in stimulating human development via cognition. Therefore, this section will explore the role of personality traits in the cognitive development of children, adolescents, and adults, especially in relation to creativity.

In one study, Premuzic-Chamorro (2006) reported that the innovative knowledge of college students at the beginning of their first academic year could predict the outcome of their academic grades four years later. This finding signifies that creative students are more likely to complete four years of college than students who are conscientious but not necessarily creative. In another study, Johnson et al. (2006) factored gender perspective into the study. The authors confirmed that boys are more creative than girls are. However, the authors were not able to predict any difference in grades of these male and female students at the end of college. However, Johnson et al. noted that male students with lower grades tended to lack personality traits and even seem to perform more poorly in school than female students did. The authors also confirmed that when students graduated from higher education institutions, the gap (Academic achievement) closed between males and females. The same authors reported that creative thinking is very important and beneficial for students in graduate school. The logical conclusion to these findings is that a combination of creativity and conscientiousness are beneficial to student academic achievement regardless of gender; however, the current assessments, which lean towards conscientiousness in the school system today, may encourage students to imitate instead of to innovate. For example, gifted students often perform well when assessments focus on creative work, rather than reproductive work or interactions with others. Examples of these unimaginative assessments include multiple-choice questions and written essay tests (Johnson et al., 2006).

Another study on creativity and conscientiousness (Driskell, Godwin, Salas, & O'Shea, 2006) reported that individuals who scored low on conscientiousness are often poor team players in an organization. The notion here is that such individuals are impulsive, irresponsible, and disorganized. Driskell et al. found that, creativity is more of an individual effort and that conscientiousness works well with group dynamics. Personality traits seem observable in teamwork dimensions, especially when an individual or a team member lacking social skills tries to maintain interpersonal relations. The individual might be very creative and be able to manage tasks and planning but lack the necessary attributes needed to resolve conflicts and maintain social-emotional relations. For example, a school principal may have all the intellectual tools to manage an inner-city public school system, but the school fails to meet the yearly performance test scores for students. When there is a lack of interpersonal relations between administrators, teachers, students, and parents, that can happen; it will take a principal who is conscientious, not creative, to raise test scores and increase students' academic achievement. In agreement with other researchers, public schools often serve as settings for people of different backgrounds, ethnicities, and cultures. Therefore, if students' test scores need to be improved, educational policy makers, including school board members, need to employ leaders who have the interpersonal skills to accomplish that goal. On the other hand, if educators want students to develop skills and strategies to become effective and productive citizens of the society, school leaders with creative minds should be retained.

In another study, Martin et al. (2009) found that creative school leaders will have a difficult time raising student test scores when compared to conscientious leaders. Martin et al.

noted that a leader is a person who leads others to do their best. In the school setting, the principal is not in the forefront of teaching and learning; the teachers and support staff are. Therefore, it is appropriate for school systems to employ conscientious leaders in place of creative ones. The enthusiastic school leader probably will be able to manage all the dynamics attributes that comes with working in a diverse environment, which will foster a sense of camaraderie among staff and faculty, which in turn may improve teaching and ultimately lead to improved student test scores.

In yet another study, Feist (2006) categorized personality traits that affect human development into three psychological domains: (a) cognitive, (b) social, and (c) motivational traits. Using the tolerance scales of the *California Psychological Inventory*, Feist explained that among cognitive traits, visionary scientists tend to be more open minded and more flexible in thought than less visionary scientists. In addition, Feist found that the more tolerant, open to experience, and flexible a student is, the more he or she will attain success over his or her lifetime. Among the social traits, Feist argued that many scientists tend to be dominant, arrogant, hostile, and self-confident. He reasoned that this finding is true because the most productive people are rewarded with more resources and that successes are for those who survive and adapt in such an environment. Feist studied the personality characteristics of biologists, chemists, and physicists in relation to their commitment to work. He reported that work productivity was very high when compared to other professionals. In addition, he noted that the groups of individuals discussed thrived on challenging and difficult tasks, enjoyed hard work, and liked competing with others. Feist also claimed that when these visionary scientists do interact with others, they often exhibit arrogance, self-confidence, and hostility. This finding may explain why many creative individuals tend to be isolated throughout their lives.

Locus of Control

In social psychology, locus of control (LOC) serves as a belief system regarding the degree to which individuals attribute success and failure. The LOC can be described as either internal or external. An internal LOC means the individual believes that he or she controls his or her life. An external LOC means the person believes that his or her environment, some higher power, or other persons control destiny (Bursik & Martin, 2006; Dilmac, Hamarta, & Arslan 2009; Martin et al., 2005; Tella, Tella, & Adeniyi, 2009; Wood, Saylor, & Cohen, 2009). Rotter (1954) was one of the early theorists that developed this framework about the LOC, and the idea has since become a remarkable part of human development studies. According to Rotter (2006), individuals with high external LOC believe that others, fate, and luck are responsible for their success or failure. Individuals with a high internal LOC believe that the outcome of an event is the result of their behavior and actions; thus, individual effort is upheld. Additionally, people with a high internal LOC have better control of their actions, tend to attribute success or failures to their effort and abilities, and are more likely to attempt to influence other people than individuals with high external LOC. Lastly, those with high internal LOC are more likely to assume that their efforts will help them be successful; are more active in seeking information and knowledge concerning their situation compared to individuals with high external LOC.

In another study, Bursik and Martin (2006) pointed out that the association of LOC for male and female adolescents is different because of maturation and socialization knowledge. The authors reported that adolescent males have a higher level of internal LOC than adolescent females. Bursik and Martin argued that high internal LOC for boys and high external LOC for girls can be the result of biological development and/or social constructs. In biological development, Bursik and Martin noted that males and females have different developmental blueprints, which are the hormonal and physical development that boys and girls experience through the stages of puberty. There is evidence that female adolescents enter the stages of puberty earlier than male adolescents do (Malina, 1990; as cited in Bursik and Martin, 2006).

Furthermore, differences in socialization experiences from childhood to adolescence may also promote gender differences in the LOC. Bursik and Martin (2006) reported that starting at an early age, girls value interpersonal relationships at a higher level than boys do. For instance, girls seemed to be exposed to the idea of following directives more than boys are. As such, girls often marry, disregard their own inner thoughts, and follow the thoughts of their new spouse. This is not wildly spread among the western culture but very distinct in many cultures, specifically third world countries. Thus, it seems logical that different socialization models, such as emotional expression, self-conception, and gender roles, may lead to the LOC an individual expresses.

Wood, Saylor, and Cohen (2009) examined the relationship between LOC and academic success among ethnically diverse baccalaureate nursing students. One hundred six baccalaureates who had completed a second semester of surgical course work participated in this study. Wood et al. surveyed students using the 45-item instrument titled *Review of Personal Effectiveness with Locus of Control* (ROPELOC) to measure self-concept and levels of personal effectiveness. Their results indicated that students who ascribed outcomes to mitigating conditions beyond their control reported external LOC and had lower grades. ESL students were also found to report external LOC. This finding indicates that a strong external LOC orientation may adversely affect academic success for nursing students. Furthermore, Wood et al. found that study strategies, persistence, and

150

supportive social connections attributed to academic success.

Wood, Saylor, and Cohen (2009) also described particularly effective study strategies that students demonstrated such as organizational skills, time management skills, working in groups, completing homework, attending classes, and reading materials ahead of time. They described persistent students as those students who worked hard, were diligent, determined, persevered, were ambitious, committed to finish the program, and exhausted their personal effort and sacrifice. Wood et al. described supportive social connections such as emotional support from family, friends, and peers in the form of love, positive attitude, and encouragement. These attributes are not inherent, or skills that individuals are born with; rather, these characteristics are conscious efforts that result from interactions with others and the environment. In addition, this study is consistent with the theory that LOC can be learned or transformed from internal to external orientation and vice versa.

In another study, it was found that LOC elements could be identified beyond the teaching and learning environment, and could also be part of relationships and attitudes used to established, maintain, and promote effectiveness in various job settings. Martin et al. (2005) reported their findings on the relationship between LOC, the quality of exchanges between subordinates and leaders, and the variety of work reactions. The researchers collected data on two samples of participants; one group consisted of 404 employees, and the other group consisted of 51 administrative staff members. Martin et al. hypothesized that people with an internal LOC developed better quality relationships with their boss compared with individual with an external LOC. In addition, internal LOC has more favorable work related issues than external LOC. The results from the study supported the authors' predictions and demonstrated the relationship between LOC and success or failure in the work environment. Failure or success was not the term the authors used. However, it appears that the lack of relationship between leaders and subordinates might then lead to termination of work, and termination of work could then lead to failure of the individual's career and goals.

In yet another study, Dilmac, Hamarta, and Arslan (2009) used the scale developed by Rotter (1966) to investigate the relationship between LOC, anxiety, avoidance, and attachment. Dilmac et al. noted that the LOC scale has a high score which signifies external LOC orientation, and having an unsatisfactory score represents an internal LOC orientation. The result of the study supported the idea that the attachment behavior of a person with external LOC shows high anxiety and avoidance more than the person with internal LOC. This finding is consistent with the knowledge that external locus of control relates to negative ego concept. In addition, Bursik and Martin (2006) found that individuals with an internal LOC can overcome negative effects on a large scale, react strongly to creative restrictions, and are impulsive and industrial. The knowledge that LOC, anxiety, and attachment styles correlated significantly indicated the importance for educators and teachers to help these individuals develop self-confidence and take responsibility for their behaviors. The inclusion of programs in the educational setting that pay attention to LOC might enable the development of healthy citizens in society.

In a similar study, Tella, Tella, and Adeniyi (2009) used Trice's academic LOC scale (1985) to examine LOC, interest in schooling, and self-efficacy as predictors of academic success of students in junior high school. Tella et al. reported that the significance of LOC on academic achievement is extremely high and cannot be overemphasized. They suggested that it is most likely that students who are not performing satisfactorily will settle for mediocre success and achievements. Furthermore, Tella et al. argued that the results imply that those academically successful students will always use LOC to improve performance. In light of these findings, there is an urgent need for students to develop internal LOC in order to correlate success to hard work. For this to be possible, students need to be taught how to set goals, both short and long term, and how to plan for the successful attainment of these goals using a specific timetable and measurable outcomes.

Neighborhoods and Schools

The neighborhood in which an individual is nurtured and raised often influences his or her human development, including biological, psychological, and social aspects as well as school success. Researchers are interested in understanding how neighborhood characteristics influence the development of children (Aviles, Anderson, & Davila, 2006; Boyle, Georgiades, Racine, & Mustard, 2007; Caughty, Murray, & O'campo, 2008; Hay, Fortson, Hollist, Altheimer and Schaible 2007; Kowasleski-Jones, Dunifon, & Ream, 2006; Moren-cross, Wright, LaGory; & Lanzi, 2006; Winslow & Shaw, 2007). These developmental issues that follow individuals from childhood through adolescence and adulthood may provide critical information regarding the negative or positive impacts of certain contexts of neighborhoods, such as poverty and prosperity. A variety of studies have scrutinized individual personalities, family relationships, school environments, and community-neighborhood interactions to describe the relationship to the healthy development of individuals. The premise presented in these studies is that the majority of children raised in affluent neighborhoods will often fare better academically, socially, and behaviorally than children in poor neighborhoods.

In one study, Boyle, Georgiades, Racine and Mustard (2007) examined the influences of neighborhood and family traits on children's scholastic achievement. Boyle et al. used multilevel models to study the longitudinal association between neighborhood and family characteristics in Ontario, Canada. They examined participants initially in 1983, when participants were between four and 16 years of age. Their findings were reported in 2001, when the participants were young adults between 22 and 23 years of age. Among their findings, affluent neighborhoods showed a high positive association with scholastic achievement. In a similar study, Boyle et al. (2007) reported that children from low-income families did not benefit academically from living in an affluent area. Thus, neighborhood characteristics alone may not affect human development. Other factors, such as family wealth, have a noticeable impact, too.

In another study carried out in the United States, Kowaleski-Jones, Dunifon, and Ream (2006) presented contrasting findings. In their investigation, they tested a model of neighborhood influence on school-aged children, including structural conditions and parental perceptions of the neighborhood. Kowaleski-Jones et al. used data from the 1990 census and the 1997 *Panel Study of Income Dynamics Child Development Supplement* (PSID-CDS). Results indicated a negative association of living in a modest community with academic success. They also reported a positive correlation for children's behavior and academic achievement when living in a community with a large immigrant population. However, there is not enough information to determine whether there is a significant finding regarding the effect of attitude and discipline on children's well being. For example, many immigrants have reported the need to give their children a better education while the opportunity is available (Nsamenang, 2008). One of the limitations to the study is that it is not longitudinal. Kowaleski-Jones did not spend time in the neighborhoods recording field notes; rather, they used data from the last census record.

Hay et al. (2007) proposed that the effects of family poverty on delinquency may strongly depend on the poverty level of the residential community. Participants were first interview in 1976 when the children were between seven and 11 years of age, with a follow-up interview conducted in 1981 when the children were between 12 and 16 years of age. The significant part of their findings was that family poverty is significant for adolescent delinquency. Poor neighborhood and family socioeconomic status creates juvenile delinquency; consequently, delinquency leads to a lack of well-being, and a substantial hindrance in individual development in a community.

In a longitudinal study, Morales and Guerra (2006) examined the effects of stress within the framework of disadvantaged schools, families, and neighborhoods. Morales and Guerra assessed participants over a two-year period. They first assessed participants when they were in grades 1-4, and then they assessed them again when they were in grades 3-6. Their findings indicated that children's achievement was highly influenced by school, family, and neighborhood stressors. In poor neighborhoods, they discovered that children from struggling families performed academically below children from more advantaged families. The effect of multiple context and cumulative stress on children is consistent with the study carried out by Boyle et al. (2007). In addition, this finding correlates with the original hypothesis that neighborhood characteristics alone do not influence the well being behavior, and academic success of children.

School environment and characteristics are noted to have the highest impact for children's well being (Aviles et al. 2006; Kowaleski-Jones et al. 2006). The school environment often has the strongest impact on children due to the amount of time they spend there. Though school might play a definite role in closing the disparity between neighborhoods, it has been noted that there is a relationship between poor neighborhoods and the schools within them (Moreen-Cross et al., 2006). Other researchers (Margolis, 2006; Winslow & Shaw, 2007) have also reported the same, eluding that the problems lies within the funding formulas that state and city governments use to finance public schools in the United States of America. For example, in some states funding of public schools comes from property tax revenue generated by each municipal government. If the property value is low, then so is the money generated by the property tax. In turn, schools located in a poor district will also serve as impoverished schools. In this case, poor communities equal poor schools due to the school funding formula of the state government. In affluent communities, the reverse is the case, to the point that because of the high value of properties, schools in the community even generate surplus funds. This study suggested that it may not be neighborhood economic status, but rather the individual situation of children living there, which is most important when predicting children's well-being. Future research should replicate these findings in more natural settings with emphasis on how to use public school education funds to bridge the gap of economic disparity between neighborhoods. In addition, municipal and state governments should find a better means to fund public schools rather than the property-value tax formula.

Cultural Influences

In western culture, the thought of children handling and playing with a knife frightens many parents. In the United States, an adolescent with a knife could be considered armed and dangerous, even to the point that the youngster may be expelled from school. However, many children in third-world countries handle knives and machetes safely. According to the same scheme, infants in many communities of the western world, sleep alone, whereas, in many third world countries, the reverse is the case. These variations in child-rearing practices show what is developmentally appropriate for children and adolescents across the globe, reflecting collective cultural difference in human development. For example, in western culture, some familiar developmental milestones in children include sleeping alone, walking and reading at certain ages, and moving from home in adulthood. In contrast, other cultures may learn to hunt, get married to many different women, and have many children. Imagine the culture shock when a westerner moves to a third world country or a third world country person moves to the western world. How does cultural variation affect the developmental of an individual, especially at the cognitive level? Could the gap in development be a product of ethnic disparity? Nsamenang (2008) stated, "Culture as in the social heritage and cultural tools, is a determinative complement of genotype that shapes humans psychosocial differentiation in the direction of a given people's cultural meaning system" (p. 73). In other words, culture could be viewed as an intelligent, desirable solution that guides different people in different periods and societies. These desirable outcomes of development can be witnessed in different countries and also within a country of autonomous beliefs and doctrinal systems (Nsamenang, 2008). Therefore, this section of paper will examine the literature in relation to the influence of culture on human development.

Social scientists and psychologists have often regarded families of non-European descent as disadvantaged in cognitive development (Feist, 2006; Lavine, 2009). Recently, the same groups of social scientists and psychologists have begun to understand the strength of ethnically diverse families and the enormous benefits for people's development. Fuller and Garcia-Coll (2010) reported the remarkable discoveries of the strengths of Latino American families regarding the development of their children. They described how a variation in culture assisted in producing social-emotional growth, cognitive development, and learning achievement for Latino American youths. The authors discovered that family cultural heritage, home language, race, and social class are crucial in the development of children. School systems need to invest time and recognize the rich social skills, respect for adults, and the tenacity by which Latino American children want to serve their family by doing well in school (Fuller & Garcia-Coll, 2010).

In yet another study, Livas-Dlott, et al. (2010) examined parental practices tied to the mother's personality among Mexican American families. They found that most Mexican American mothers relied on low assertive methods with verbal commands, instead of inductive strategies that involved reasoning. They also reported that only insignificant compliance required punitive strategies. Livas-Dlott et al. noted that the reliance on verbal prompts and other tools used by the mother depends on the education and acculturation levels of the mother. Cultural perspective also plays a crucial role in how Mexican American mothers raise their children, compared to

European American mothers (Feist, 2006; Fuller & Garcia Coll, 2010; Livas-Dlott et al. 2010). For example, Mexican American mothers require children to follow and respect adult authority, parents and peers and to help out in household chores, compared to European American mothers, whose emphasis focuses on children's autonomy and moderate participation in household tasks (Fuller & Garcia-Coll, 2010). These cultural differences in child rearing do not necessarily place one style above the other; rather, cultural sensitivity needs to be employed by various agencies, such school systems where children of different backgrounds are taught and nurtured.

In another study, Wood, Saylor, and Cohen (2009) examined the relationship between LOC and academic success among ethnically diverse nursing students. The academic success was a match with high grade point average, medical-surgical theory grades, and standardized medical-surgical test scores. In addition, ethnicity correlated with culture, and academic success linked with appropriate human development. Their findings showed statistical significance in the differences among ethnic groups for external LOC. In addition, they found that ESL students had a higher external LOC than other students. Wood et al. argued that perhaps one could attribute internal LOC to western culture and thinking, whereas external LOC is tied to Eastern philosophies.

Some researchers have also linked the external LOC phenomenon with negative racial stereotyping and lack of academic performance among African American, Latino American students, and other immigrants (Aso, 2008; Smith & Hopkins, 2004 as cited in Wood et al. 2009). Beyond ethnicity and the racial disparity that exits in the United States, cultural beliefs and customs provide the stage for the development of intelligence and other valued traits for the well being of children worldwide (Fuller & Garcia Coll, 2010). For example, children's language development is often improved by the rich verbal interactions with their mother in the context of doing household chores in many non-westerner households (Livas-Dlott at el. 2010). Many of these cultural perspectives, or tools, are lost or not used significantly during the crucial developmental stages of children from diverse backgrounds. Super and Harkness (2008) argued that these cultural tools are lost due to the subtle intrusion of western beliefs and values that dominate the society derived from western-oriented education. In summary, public organizations, such as the school system that play an enormous role in human cognitive development, need to include various culturally sensitive curricula and activities to provide a multitude of benefits towards children's development.

This section of paper combined the human development constructs of theorists such as Piaget, Bandura, and Egan with current research studies on the cognitive development of a person from birth to adulthood. Included in this discussion was the role of personality traits,

LOC, neighborhoods, schools, and cultures in relation to adolescent development. Since there are no special directions to raise a child, people often follow their own style. One's culture or heritage, social economic status, or even the nature of the neighborhood in which they reside may be factors that influence the cognitive development of children and adolescents.

At the beginning of this section, a question was posed about why children fair differently in relation to academic success in school. The findings in the literature support the need for school systems and parents to collaborate much more in order to increase the well being of children and adolescents. This need is strong, since children spend most of their quality time in schools. In addition, different cultural perspectives were also reported as one of the disparities in human development. In this case, the school systems can level the playing fields in offering each child and adolescent what is the norm for each environment. For instance, mainstream development in Western culture might be different from that of Eastern or Middle Eastern cultures. What if a child migrates with his or her family from an Asian country to the United States? The child will not learn about his family's way of life in any American schools; rather, the child will learn more about the Western culture. This emphasis on Western culture will unquestionably create conflict between the child and parents as the child develops in the Western world. This conflict can also create emotional and stressful issues for the developing child, which might lead to emotional instability due to a lack of parental support. In this situation, the Asian parents need to be part of the school and to collaborate with the school through the Parent Teacher Organization (PTO) in order to share Asian values with the school system. This example is not limited to Asian students; the school should expand this knowledge base throughout the school depending on the diversity of the school.

It is true that children will often persevere, regardless of any obstacle in front of their path toward full human development. However, strong parental involvement in public schools, better neighborhoods, and sensitivity or accommodation of other cultures will improve and shape human development in children, regardless of family background and wealth. It is up to the adults to take the necessary steps to provide a nurturing environment for children to thrive and succeed. When children thrive and achieve, they in turn become good contributors to society.

APPLICATION II

Professional Practice and Human Development in Education

Section III served as a foundation for the application section of this paper by examining some major theorists in human development and the impact of their work on the field of education today. Section IV presented an investigation of current research in human development, particularly in relation to cognitive development in children and adolescents. In examining the most recent work of researchers (Caughy, Nettles, & O'Campo, 2008; Fuller, & Garcia Coll, 2010; Nsamenang, 2008), it was clear that changing the approach to raising children as a community might sustain effective processes that fit the models prescribed by Piaget, Bandura, and Egan. Creating an environment that allows children to be equal and meeting the needs of every individual to help them develop effectively and properly is one theme that kept surfacing during the paper reviews. Good neighborhoods, acceptance of diversity, and exemplary schools all play an enormous role in the development of children and adolescents. Therefore, the section III and IV portions of this paper support the notion that attention to children's well being can serve as a robust base for human development.

The purpose of this application section is to present a project that combines the theoretical constructs of the section III component and the current research of the section IV component. This project will describe the professional development sessions that were used to provide educators with the knowledge and implementation of healthy habits of mind, which enhances student learning and cognitive growth among adolescent learners. In addition, this section will present a protocol that focuses on modeling habits of mind for adolescent learners in public high schools in order to lower dropout rates. Teachers at Any School USA received this professional development session through a power point slide show that included real lesson plans on the habits of mind of a successful high school student, a model borrowed from the Vermont Department of Education (2005). In addition, included in this document are sections describing, the project rationale and the content of the project. A conclusion will also be presented.

Project Rationale

This professional development session, which was presented for faculty members at Any School USA, was an effort to help teachers and school administrators improve services to children who are developmentally different from their peers. Fuller and Garcia-Coll (2010) reported that children in today's school system are much more diverse culturally different from children of previous years. Could this diversity and differences in culture be the reason for the dissimilarity in cognitive levels in adolescents? Based on the literature about culture, diversity, and human development, one can conclude that families raise children differently because of cultural differences. In addition, poor neighborhoods seem to have slight impact on adolescent development. However, family wealth had the most negative impact in human development (Nsamenang, 2008).

Many students can be considered new to Western culture. Because this is the case, teachers have to work harder to eliminate disparities in the culture by being culturally sensitive to students of nonwestern cultures. The federal, state, and municipal governments need to find ways to close the economic disparity within the community. For example, municipal governments, through the assistance of the federal government, could use grants to modernize certain neighborhoods with large immigrant populations. Furthermore, schools in poor neighborhoods could be properly funded to equalize educational opportunities for all children. Thus, faculty members at Any School USA were the recipients of this application project in order to become aware of this gap in cognitive development and to consider ways to bridge that gap. The hope is that teachers might change their style, perhaps even incorporate certain cultures, in order to help students acclimate to Western norms.

Project Plan

The professional development session began with the Dean of Students welcoming teachers and introducing the presenter and his role as a former teacher and educational researcher. During the introduction, the presenter asked the participants to write the words "entrance ticket" on a piece of paper, and he then requested participants to write what their expectations were for the professional development session. He collected these written responses for reference in relation to future professional development sessions. In an effort to connect the content of the session with the participants' lives, both professional and personal, the presenter shared an anecdote about his experience as a student in relation to certain habits of mind that were expected of him in high school. Participants were then asked to introduce themselves including their name, classroom location, and subject taught. After introductions, participants were asked to share one thing they knew about the habits of high school students and what role they might play in improving these habits. As each participant introduced an idea, the presenter led a discussion around any related issues relevant to the discussion. During this discussion, many of the concepts evident in the section III and IV of this paper surfaced. Following this opening discussion, content was introduced, beginning with a review of human development, including the developmental stages as described in the theories of Piaget and Egan. These theories were explicitly related to human cognitive development through a discussion of the contemporary contributions of Aviles et al. (2006), Bursik, and Martin (2006), Chamorro-Premuzic (2006), Feist (2006), and Nsamenang (2008). Based on research from section III portion of this paper, participants were introduced to the developmental theories of Piaget, Bandura, and Egan. In addition to the work of these theorists, the research of Fuller and Garcia Coll (2010) on differences in culture and the work of Moren-Cross et al. (2006) on neighborhood characteristics and problem behavior among disadvantaged children were addressed.

Following the overview, a more in-depth discussion of each theorist began. Participants were asked to recall and share their prior knowledge of Piaget, and many participants were able to share a great deal. The presenter then focused on Piaget's (1969) belief that children and adolescents were not limited to receiving information and knowledge from parents or educators; instead, they actively construct their own knowledge. Following a discussion of cognitive development, the presenter also focused on Piaget's (1969) discussion of the role of education in human cognitive development. The presenter pointed out that Piaget's cognitive development theory did not include formal education as part of the framework of the developmental stages. The presenter emphasized to the group that children would not reach any stage of cognitive development without proper education or guidance. Organized education is well suited to improve cognitive abilities, for instance, when comparing human beings to other animals, because only humans understand and are able to do what they have learned. Bandura (1986) agreed that such knowledge might come from observations or modeling, processes which are often used in teaching and learning in public school systems. Throughout the discussion of Piaget's cognitive development theory, participants drew parallels to the work of Bandura and Egan. At this point, the presentation turned from discussing individual theorists in human development to a discussion of the application project. This

169

section of the presentation began with a brief overview of the habits of mind created by the Vermont Department of Education (2005). Costa and Kallick (2005) noted that the 16 habits of mind are habits of thought and action that help people manage uncertain or challenging situations. These habits of mind can help people take action when there is no known solution to a problem. Costa and Kallick argued that these habits of mind also support thoughtful and intelligent action and include the following:

1. Thinking about thinking
2. Remaining open to continuous learning
3. Thinking flexibly
4. Persisting
5. Finding humor
6. Striving for accuracy
7. Listening with understanding and empathy
8. Gathering data through all the senses
9. Thinking and communicating with clarity and precision
10. Thinking interdependently
11. Creating, imagining, and innovating
12. Responding with wonderment and awe
13. Applying past knowledge to new situations
14. Questioning and posing problems
15. Managing impulsivity
16. Taking responsible risks

This discussion of the habits of mind was followed by a power point presentation explaining and narrating each of the sixteen habits of mind for high school students. At the end of the presentation, the presenter recommended that participants use what they had learned to run advisory classes for their students. The presenter modeled a lesson plan for participants on how to introduce the habits of mind to students and how to create habits of mind portfolio. The presenter assigned participants to 16 groups of not less than three people in a group. Each group was encouraged to complete a basic lesson plan on the assigned habits of mind. After groups have developed a lesson plan, the presenter encouraged individuals from groups to rotate, create a new group, and share a lesson plan with the new group. This rotation continued until all participants were able to share their lesson plans. Participants were encouraged to ask questions about the presentation. Participants were also requested to complete an exit ticket describing what was learned, what worked, and what did not work. The entrance and exit tickets were personal notes for the presenter to use in order to evaluate the presentation. In tallying the evaluation, 100% of the participants strongly agreed that the presenter demonstrated knowledge of the subject matter and was well prepared and organized. One hundred percent also agreed, or strongly agreed, that the presenter was able to inspire interest and respond to participant needs. Several participants left enthusiastic and positive comments such as "Great class! Good resources!" and "The presenter was very knowledgeable about the subject matter. Thank you for your time!!! I enjoyed the presentation!" When asked how the session could have been improved, some participants shared constructive suggestions as well. This session may be offered again as an on-going professional development session for teachers, and an emphasis would be on the use of advising in education. The feedback from participant evaluations was valuable in relation to the presenter's effort to improve the session for future events.

Theory to Practice

Section III of this book presented an analysis of some of the theories of human development, with a focus on the works of Piaget, Bandura, and Egan. This theory was put into practice through the application part of the book, during which participants received and discussed information during the first segment of the professional development session. Participants might now incorporate this theory into their teaching practices using awareness, experience, and imagination in their classes. Section IV of the book was a critical examination of the cognitive development of children and adolescents in relation to the theories of human cognitive development presented in the breadth section. In the professional development session of the application component, participants were given the opportunity to apply the theories and current research in relation to cognitive development in children and adolescents (Aviles et al., 2006; Bursik, & Martin, 2006; Chamorro-

Premuzic, 2006; Feist, 2006; and Nsamenang, 2008) in their classrooms. Along with section III and IV portions, the application portion also supports the argument that cognitive development in children and adolescents can be improved in formal K-12 educational systems. The application portion also provided participants with hands-on activities to assist them with the practical application of these cognitive development theories. Finally, participants were introduced to a variety of ways to apply these theories in their own classrooms, including the use of cooperative learning, multicultural education, and role-playing. Ultimately, the focus was on the potential power of teaching and learning to serve as developmental learning tools to improve the cognitive skills of children and adolescents and as instruments of positive change in education. The hope was that participants would apply these cognitive development theories in their distinctive roles as educators, ensuring that the future will be a better place for children and adolescents.

Appendix: A
Sample Lesson Plan
(Modified from the Vermont Department of Education)
Teaching Habits of Mind
Lesson 1: Introduction to the Habits of Mind and Habits of the Mind Portfolio
1 hour
Lesson Objectives:
- Students will describe habits of mind in their own words.
- Students will understand how to build habits of mind portfolio.

Provide an overview of the course and how to build a portfolio. Participants will use a word splash to describe each habit in their own words. This activity gives students a chance to think about each habit and define it in personal terms.

Materials:
- Newsprint and markers or individual papers and markers for small group
- Paper and fine-tip markers
- Word splash and walkabout poster session

This lesson is taught using a word splash during a walkabout poster session. A word splash is a collection of key terms, synonyms, and phrases that convey meanings similar to a particular term. It enhances fluency with the terms and elaborates their meaning. A word splash also enhances flexibility by providing a group of terms rather than restricting someone to the use of a single term.

A walkabout poster session is an opportunity for participants to get up and move. Moving is important for people who may have difficulty sitting still for long periods for a variety of reasons. This activity also enables people to participate actively in a variety of ways. Students who are not verbal learners or are less articulate can draw symbols or participate actively by reading what others write. Walking about also helps people mix with people they do not know.

Place posters labeled with each habit on the walls around the room. Give each participant a marker. Ask participants to walk about and stop at each poster. Think of a word or short phrase that describes each habit for them and add it to the list. Participants are not required to have a word for each habit, but are encouraged to add one. They are expected to stop by each poster and think about what the habit means to them and look at what other people have written.

After everyone has completed a walkabout, regroup and read the lists. Ask for any additional words the group would like to add.

Participants were also reminded to find other ways of teaching this unit. For example, providing alternative approaches for students who find writing challenging, such as recording journal entries on a tape recorder, use art or story boards to express what they learn, schedule periodic interviews with students, or write raps or songs. The objective would be met if students reflect on each habit, try it out, and reflect on how they use it. The portfolio should be progressive, and students should continue to reflect on all habits as they begin to use them in combination with each other.

References

Aviles, M. A., Anderson, T. R., & Davila, E. R. (2006). Child and adolescent social-emotional development within the context of school. *Child and Adolescent Mental Health, 11*(1), 32-39.

Bandura, A. (1986). *Social foundations of thought and action: A social cognitive theory.* Englewood Cliffs, NJ: Prentice Hall.

Boyle, M. H., Georgiades, K., Mustard, C., & Racine, Y. (2007). Neighborhood and family influences on educational attainment: Results from the Ontario child health study follow-up, 2001. *Child Development, 78*(1), 168-189.

Bursik, K., & Martin, T. A. (2006). Ego development and adolescent academic achievement. *Journal of Research on Adolescence, 16*(1), 1-18.

Chamorro-Premuzic, T. (March, 2006). Creativity versus conscientiousness: which is better predictor of student performance? *Applied Cognitive Psychology, 20*, 521-531.

Costa, A.L, & Garmston, R. J. (2002). *Cognitive coaching: a foundation for renaissance schools* (2nd ed.). Norwood, MA: Christopher-Gordon.

Caughy, O.M.; Nettles, S.M; & O'Campo, P.J. (July, 2008). The effect of residential neighborhood on child behavior problems in first grade. *American Journal Community Psychology, 42,* 39-50.

Caughy, O.M.; Nettles, S.M.; O'Campo, P.J.; Lohrfink, K.F. (2006). Neighborhood matters: racial socialization of African American children. *Child Development, 77*(5), 1220-1236.

Egan, K. (1997). *The educated mind: How cognitive tools shape our understanding.* Chicago: University of Chicago Press.

Feist, G. J. (2006). How development and personality influence scientific thought, interest, and achievement. *Review of General Psychology, 10*(2), 163-182.

Fuller, B. & Garcia-Coll, C. (2010). Learning from Latinos: contexts, families, and child development in motion. *Developmental Psychology, 46*(3), 559-565.

Habits of Mind Curriculum - Print Version. (2005). Retrieved June 2, 2010 from http://doc.vermont.gov/programs/educational-programs/wdp-materials/habits-of-mind-curriculum

Hay, C.; Fortson, N.; Hollist, D.R.; Altheimer, I; & Schaible, L.M. (March, 2007). Compound risk: The implications for delinquency of coming from a poor family that lives in a poor community. *Journal Youth Adolescence, 36,* 593-605.

Higgins, M. (2009, May). Standardized tests: wristwatch or dipstick? *Research in Education, 81,* 1-11.

Hunt, G.H; Wiseman, D.G and Touzel, T.M. (2009). *Effective teaching: preparation and implementation* (4th ed.). Springfield, IL: Charles C Thomas.

Hunter, M. (1994). *Enhancing teaching.* New York: Macmillan College.

Hunter, R. (2004). *Mastery teaching: increasing instructional effectiveness in elementary and secondary schools.* Thousand Oaks, CA: Sage.

Johnson, W.; McGue, M.; & Iacono, G. W. (2006). Genetic and environmental influences on academic achievement trajectories during adolescence. *Developmental Psychology, 42*(3), 514-532.

Kalyuga, S.; (2006). Assessment of learner's organized knowledge structures in adaptive learning environment. *Applied Cognitive Psychology, 20;* 333-342.

Kowaleski-Jones, L.; Dunifan, R.; & Ream, G. (2006). Community contributions to scholastic success. *Journal of Community Psychology, 34*(3), 343-362.

Livas-Dlott, A.; Fuller, B.; Stein, G., Bridges, M.; Figueroa, M.A.; & Mireles, L. (2010). Commands, competence, and carino: maternal socialization practices in Mexican American families. *Developmental Psychology, 46*(3), 566-578.

Margolis, J. (2006). New teachers, high-stakes diversity, and the performance-based conundrum. *The Urban Review, 38*(1), 27-44.

Marieb, E. (2003). *Essentials of human anatomy and physiology.* (7th ed.). San Francisco, Benjamin Cummings.

Marzano, R.J., Pickering, J.D., & Pollock, J.E. (2001). *Classroom instruction that works: research based strategies for increasing student achievement.* Alexandria, VA: Association for supervision and curriculum development.

Meier, L.S.; Rich, S.B.; & Cady, J. (2006). Teacher's use of rubrics to score non-traditional tasks: factors related to discrepancies in scoring. *Assessment in Education, 13*(1), 69-95.

McLean, K. C. & Pratt, M. W. (2006). Life's little (and Big) lessons: Identity statuses and meaning-making in the turning point narratives of emerging adults. *Developmental Psychology, 42*(4), 714-722.

Morales, J. R.; & Guerra, N. G. (2006). Effects of multiple context and cumulative stress on urban children's adjustment in elementary school. *Child Development, 77*(4), 907-923.

Moren-Cross, L.J.; Wright, D. R.; LaGory, M.; & Lanzi, G.R. (2006). Percieved neighborhood characteristics and problem behavior among disadvantaged children. *Child Psychiatry and Human Development, 36*(3), 273-294.

Nsamenang, B.A. (2008). Culture and human development. *International Journal of Psychology, 43*(2), 73-77.

Olina, Z.; Reiser, R. Huang, X.; Lim, J.; & Park, S. (2006). Problems format and presentation sequence: effects on learning and mental effort among US high school students. *Applied Cognitive Psychology, 20*; 299-309.

Pacini-Ketchabaw, V. (2006). Perspective on child and adolescent development: challenges and possibilities for teaching. *Relational Child and Youth Care practice, 21*(3), 39-42.

Pettit, S. G., Davis-Kean, P. E., Magnuson, K. (2009). Educational attainment in developmental perspective: longitudinal analyses of continuity, change, and process. *Merrill-Palmer Quarterly*, 55(3), 217–223.

Piaget, J. (1977). *The development of thought: Equilibration of cognitive structure.* New York: Viking Press.

Piaget, J. & Inhelder, B. (1969). *The psychology of the child.* New York: Basic Books.

Pillow, B. H. (2008). Development of children's understanding of cognitive activities. The *Journal of Genetic Psychology, 169*(4), 297-321.

Posner, G. J. (2004). Analyzing the curriculum. (3rd ed.). New York: McGraw Hill.

Schneider, J.; Ramsay, A.; & Lowerson, S. A. (2006). Sure start graduates: predictors of attainment on starting school. *Child Care, Health & Development, 32*(40, 431-440.

Staudt, B.; & Neubauer, A.C. (2006). Achievement, underachievement and cortical activation: a comparative EEG study of adolescents of average and above-average intelligence. *High Ability Studies, 17*(1), 3-16.

Stoeger, H. (2006). First steps towards an epistemic learner model. *High Ability Studies, 17*(1), 17-41.

Tella, A.; Tella, A.; & Adeniyi, O. (October, 2009). Locus of control, interest in schooling, self efficacy and academic achievement. *Cypriot Journal of Educational Sciences, 4,* 168-182.

Thompson, C. (2009, May). Preparation, practice, and performance An empirical examination of the impact of Standards-based Instruction on secondary students' math and science achievement. *Research in Education, 81,* 53-62.

Winslow, E.B.; & Shaw, D.S. (April, 2007). Impact of neighborhood disadvantage on overt behavior problems during early childhood. *Aggressive Behavior, 33,* 207-219.

Wood, M.A.; Saylor, C.; and Cohen, J. (2009). Locus of control and academic success among ethically diverse baccalaureate nursing students. *Nursing Education Perspectives, 30*(5), 290-294.

SECTION V

Theories of Structural Thinking in Education

All systems have several purposes, including increase productivity, to serve people effectively and efficiently, and to better relationships. Whether the systems are educational institutions or organizations, problems arise that require certain structural solutions. All systems have one ending purpose, which is to improve relationships and increase productivity? The system, as a whole, must look at the entire structure, instead of the individual components to be successful in determining the plan of action, which needs to be accomplished. For example, in terms of educational systems, mission statements are the key. Each part of the system functions independently in the plan of action. This relationship between the parts to the whole is known as systems thinking.

According to Wheatley (1999), systems thinking assume a revolutionary paradigm, which views the world as organizations, wholes, or systems, not as mechanical models in which life is an accidental product of physical processes or appears as a product of chance. Senge (2006) argued that a system can be defined as an organized collection of unified elements distinguished by a boundary and a functional unit. According to Hoy and Miskel (1978), a system includes the individuals and their roles; the purpose, goals, and functions; the hierarchy of levels; the individual components; the system boundaries in the environment; and the systems diagram of the structure and relationship to the environment. The behaviors of the system need to be observed in the form of strategies and tactics, surprises, and the ability of the system to succeed and sustain itself.

Consequently, several systems theorists have developed theories relating to systems thinking. This section will analyze the work of system thinkers such as Peter Senge, Hoy and Miskel, and Margaret Wheatley. Furthermore, this paper will describe the contributions of these theories of systems thinking to educational organizations in today's society.

Senge's Learning Organization

Senge's (2006) book titled *The Fifth Discipline: The Art and Practice of the Learning Organization* focused on business environments, mainly large corporations. However, some of his ideas resonate in educational environments as well. Senge (1990) claimed that the most successful organization is one in which members of the organization are constantly learning, in what he called "the learning organization" (p.126). The style of the learning organization asks each member of an organization to embrace change; even though individuals are working towards personal growth and success, they should also think about the whole organization and how they contribute to the success of the organization. Senge noted that humans love to learn and learning is part of peoples' DNA; thus, organizations that are highly successful are those in which its members are constantly learning to learn.

Educational systems also share the same analogy but in a more definite and profound way. For example, schools are living learning organizations; however, the learning tends to be directed at students. In Senge's learning organization theory, K-12 school systems share the same analogy with large companies; the only striking difference is one is for profit and the other is non-profit. When applied to schools, Senge's theory requires that all individuals involved in the school business need to be a part of the learning scheme. In order words, administrators, teachers, parents, custodians, and food service works must be part of the learning in the school system.

In the process of guiding organizations to continuously improve their capabilities to reach their highest goals, Senge (2006) developed five protocols that organizations could adopt to become successful learning organizations. These five protocols are known as the disciplines of the learning organization, and they include systems thinking, personal mastery, mental models, building shared vision, and team learning. Though these disciplines were developed for business environments, they can also be employed in any organization where groups of people work for a common goal. Each of the five disciplines provides an important element in developing an organization that can learn and build competence to succeed at the highest level.

Systems Thinking

Senge (2006) argued that systems thinking consists of the endeavors people do at work that contribute to the efficient functioning of the organization. Senge claimed that these individual endeavors are invisible and sometimes do not seem to count yet those activities or roles are vital to the survival of the organization. Senge argued that systems thinking are the method of understanding how these five disciplines work together within the whole organization. In K-12 school systems, systems thinking include the environment in which groups such as administrators, students, teachers, and parents work together to improve student achievement. In an organization such as public school system; people, structures, and processes work together to make the school viable for teaching and learning.

Systems thinking; as proposed by Senge (1990), are seen as an approach to problem solving, by viewing the issues in an organization as parts of an overall system, instead of focusing on a specific part, outcomes, or events. Systems thinking are not one entity, but rather a set of routines, rituals, and practices within a structure that is based on the belief that the various parts of a system may be understood in the context of interaction with each other and with other systems, instead of in isolation. Senge contended that systems thinking deals with understanding a system by investigating the pattern of connections and interactions between the people and activities that make up the whole

187

system. An improvement in one area of an organization can unfavorably affect another area of the organization, and systems thinking promote communication at all levels in order to avoid problems. For example, the custodian may not be a known part of the learning scheme in a school organization, but he or she could be part of the system by re-directing an unruly student and contacting either a teacher or the principal about the student's behavior.

In essence, systems thinking are ways of assisting individuals to examine an organization from a wider view, which includes seeing the overall structures, patterns, and cycles in a system, rather than seeing only specific events in the system. For example, in a school system, a teacher may often use instructional strategies without collaborating with other content area teachers. Using Senge's theory of systems thinking, teachers would begin to collaborate to build a stronger instructional program. This idea could be applied to all instructional programs within a K-12 system. This extensive view of the system can help principals and school policy makers to quickly identify the real causes of issues in schools, such as low-test scores, and know where to work to address them. Senge (2006) argued that systems thinking have created a method for analyzing and changing organizations.

Personal Mastery

Another one of the five disciplines, according to Senge (2006), is personal mastery. Senge suggested that personal mastery is not achieving dominance over people or things. He emphasized that personal mastery is the act of acquiring maximum proficiency in an individual's quest. Senge argued that organizations learn from the learning of individual members. Nevertheless, this individual learning does not guarantee organizational success. Senge claimed that people with personal mastery are capable of achieving success in things that matter the most. According to Senge, individuals with personal mastery approach every situation just like an artist would approach a work of art. They accomplish personal mastery by total commitment to lifelong learning, no matter what the circumstances. As Senge noted," Personal mastery is the discipline of continually clarifying and deepening our personal vision, of focusing our energies, of developing patience, and of seeing reality objectively" (p.7). The idea of personal mastery involves clarifying things that matter the most and living life to the utmost.

Senge also made several recommendations in relation to personal mastery. The first recommendation is to constantly clarify what is important, and the second recommendation is to continually learn how to see reality more clearly. To address these recommendations, Senge used vision and reality as a metaphor to explain how individuals could acquire personal mastery. Vision, he explained, includes what individuals want and reality represents where individuals are relative to their vision, that is, what people want. Senge described the gap or distance between an individual's vision and current reality as the obstacle to successfully acquiring personal mastery. He called the gap "creative tension" or "creative energy" (p.151). Creative tension occurs when a person fails to close the gap between vision and current reality; on the other hand, creative energy is when someone learns to check current reality as he or she carries out his or her vision. According to Senge, people who achieve proficiency in personal mastery are the ones who reduce the gap between vision and reality.

In explaining this meaning of vision, Senge (2006) insisted on differentiating individual purpose and vision. He argued that purpose is a specific direction whereas vision is more a picture of the future. In addition, Senge used the terms *abstract* and *concrete* to describe the relationship between purpose and vision. He explained that abstract in place of purpose is what a person thinks about, but is not yet attained, and concrete is that which can be seen, touched, or smelled, an accomplished idea. For example, the purpose of education is served when a school system assumes the responsibility for educating students. However, when school systems hope to graduate 90% of their senior class successfully each year, this is the school vision.

Concerning creative tension, Senge (2006) noted that creative tension is the gap generated between one's vision and one's reality. He described creative tension as those things that hinder individual progress and accomplishments. This gap can make a vision unrealistic or bizarre; it can also be discouraging and make one feel hopeless. Senge used a stretched rubber band as a metaphor to describe the relationship between vision and current reality. He explained that when a rubber band is stretched with two hands, positioning both hands upside down, one on top of the other, and the hand on top is the vision and the one below is the current reality. The rubber band, when stretched, creates tension. To interpret the metaphor, Senge asked, "What does a stretched rubber band want?" (p. 150). He acknowledged that the rubber band needs release or resolution, and the only two possible ways to solve this problem is to pull the current reality toward the vision or to pull the vision toward the current reality. The metaphor could also correlate to what people do every day. Whenever individuals try to create a vision that is not aligned with current reality, creative tension pops up. Senge suggested that creative tension could be called anxiety or stress; therefore, creative tension could lead to emotions associated with anxiety, such as sadness, discouragement, hopelessness, and worry. However, Senge noted that these negative emotions are not associated with creative tension, but rather with emotional tension. He insisted that if individuals fail to separate creative tension from emotional tension, there is likelihood that the vision will be lowered.

Mental Models

Senge (2006) believed that mental models are generalizations, assumptions, and mental images of human understanding of the world and how individuals take action to resolve issues. The models, he claimed, are at the subconscious level, and the impact that they have on human behaviors are very visible. That is to say, mental models have a profound effect on the way humans view the world. The same mental models also shape human behavior toward objects and things around them. The use of mental models could lead to many human biases and wrong assumptions; that is, if the mental image or the assumption is not lifted from the subconscious level to the conscious level, people might be in conflict with one another.

Senge (2006) claimed that an individual mental model locked in the subconscious level is responsible for most human conflict. He argued that conflicts exist in the way that individuals seem to make unintended generalizations about others. Senge also insisted that these conflicts are in part due to what people say and how people behave. According to Senge, these assumptions and generalizations created by human thinking and behavior are never communicated directly to one another. For example, staff members in a school might believe that the principal thinks a teacher is incompetent, but often they will not ask the principal directly about his or her thoughts concerning this teacher. The staff members continue to work with the teacher even though the problem lingers. Senge argued that human should use every effort to bring their thoughts and behavior to a conscious level when dealing with one another. This direct thinking is primarily important in the work place, such as the school system, where groups of diverse people interact.

Senge (2006) claimed managing mental models at a personal and interpersonal level involves reflection and inquiry skills. Reflection skills are concerned with the need for individuals to slow down their thinking processes in order to be aware of their mental models. On the other hand, inquiry skills deal with how individuals interact or behave with others in a variety of situations, often in dealing with difficult and confrontational matter. This idea is what individuals assume when something happens and immediately a generalization, and a conclusion is drawn. Senge called this conclusion a "leap of abstraction" (p.192); he argued that the conscious mind is often not equipped to deal with concrete elements; thus, the rational mind replaces simple concepts with assumptions in reference to these concepts. The tendency to generalize and create innuendo and turn them into truths without investigation or clarification is considered a leap of abstraction. These assumptions create indifferences, which prevent the development of better relationships. Senge believed that individuals could avoid these leaps of abstraction by taking the time to question generalizations and assumptions and separating them from the information that led to them in the first place.

Shared Vision

Senge (2006) explained that shared vision is a sense of commonality that every member of an organization carries at heart. The vision spreads like a plague throughout the organization and gives consistency to a variety of activities within the system. For a vision to be truly shared, all members of an organization must have a similar picture and commit to having the same picture, not necessarily to an individual having it. When people share a vision, they are connected, bound together with common goal. Senge believed that shared vision is the reason why people come together to purse a specific ambition. Compliance, not commitment, is seen in many organizations without shared vision. Senge insisted that the vision found in organizations is more one person's vision and is often imposed on members by the leader of the organization, rather than a vision shared by all.

In an organization, shared vision changes how individuals relate to the organization. Senge (2006) noted that shared vision creates an atmosphere where people who distrust each other work together; at least, it is the first step that allows people with the same sense of purpose to work together. Senge also noted that members of the team start seeing the company as "our company" instead of "their company". In this regard, Senge argued, "in fact, an organization's shared sense of purpose, vision, and operating values establish the most basic level of commonality." (p. 208).

Although Senge (2006) referenced specific companies and large corporations, the idea of a learning organization is not limited to businesses. The learning organization also applies to school systems, especially the K-12 educational environment. When Senge noted that the learning organization is unable to exist without shared vision, this statement resonates for educational systems today. School systems are charged with teaching and learning and creating future adults (Hunter, 1994). It is clear that for schools to accomplish this purpose or mission, shared vision becomes everyone's business. Shared vision challenges deeply held views and opens individual ways of thinking and acting and recognizing personal and group shortcomings. Fritz (cited in Senge, 2006) commented, "In the presence of greatness, pettiness disappears. In the absence of a great dream, pettiness prevails." (p. 209).

Team Learning

Imagine any competition that requires groups of people coming together for a common goal, which is to win or succeed. For example, soccer teams have to plan, practice, and execute together in order to win games. Senge (2006) noted that what happens when individual members of the team opt to do their own thing in order to look good at the expense of the other members, they often generate chaos. In this scenario, Senge argued, a relationship needs to exist for members of a team in order to learn and be effective and in order to create sustainable success year after year. Senge's ideas involve common sense, but these ideas would not be noticed in an organization that functions as a team unless learning in the organization is collectively shared as every person's responsibility.

Some of the major ideas generated by Senge include alignment before empowerment, individual action versus reality, dialogue versus discussion, building collegiality rather than competition, defensive routines that lead to symptomatic solutions, and team rehearsal. In relation to alignment before empowerment, Senge (2006) described the need for individuals in a team to abandon their personal achievement and focus on group success, or what he called "alignment before empowerment" (p. 235). Doing so would lead groups of people to function as a whole, therefore creating what Senge called an "alignment" (p. 234). Learning to work together is the key to alignment. Senge noted that working together allows individuals to be able to attain success as individuals, too. For example, even though the individual is successful, the failures of the organization affect the person's overall success. Senge suggests that individuals need to work for the greater good of the team before working on individual vision. Furthermore, he claimed that when individuals work for the team vision, there is the likelihood that the collective shared vision aligns with the individual vision, thereby creating success for the individual and for the organization.

In relation to individual action versus reality, Senge (2006) argued that individual actions in a team create the reality for all to develop improved relationships with one another. The idea is that members in a team need to learn how to work together regardless of personalities and petty conflicts that arise in a group. Senge insisted on the need for a team to coordinate every action. For example, a basketball team needs to work as a team to perform in unprompted, yet synchronized ways. Senge believed that other groups that work as a team create the same type of relationship or what he called an "operational trust". In this trust, each team member is openly aware of other team members and can be trusted to behave in ways that match or add to each other's actions in a positive manner.

Senge (2006) pointed out that problems that exist in team learning often arise due to individual actions that are guided by individual perceptions. He noted that thoughts are not productive until people learn to examine others peoples' thoughts, including their own. In order to examine other peoples' ideas in a team, the team needs to develop protocols that allow an encouraging environment to exist. This environment will create opportunities for what Senge called "dialogue and discussion" (p.241), which should be carried out without any underlying agendas or vendettas among the people in an organization. For example, dialogue calls for each person to bring forth an idea without being interrupted or challenged by another person. That is, the person listening should not say a word. Discussion comes after dialogue, and in this regard, each idea or thought needs to be examined by all members first for commonality. In other words, Senge agreed that the need for individuals in an organization to learn how to listen to one another carefully without being judgmental is the first step in team learning. Senge emphasized the idea that teams in an organization who use dialogue and discussion effectively build strong successful organizations where collegiality exists rather than competition.

Furthermore, Senge (2006) noted that an organization that lacks the use of dialogue and discussion creates stagnant behavior among members of the team. He called this behavior "defensive routines" (p.251). In addition, Senge insisted that defensive routines lead to symptomatic solutions, in which members of an organization become compliant, not innovative and committed visionaries. In summary, Senge noted that teams could become strong and successful if the members learn to work together to achieve the organization's vision. This practice he called "team rehearsal" (p.259). Senge insists that a successful team in any organization needs to rehearse just like championship teams do in order to win games.

Hoy and Miskel's Educational Administration Theory

In their book titled *Educational Administration: Theory, Research, and Practice,* Hoy and Miskel (1978) contend that a school is a social system and at the same time a learning organization. They claimed that the accomplishment of a vision requires efforts from groups of people; individuals come together to deliberately create an organization to oversee activities and develop enticements and rewards that encourage others to join them in their quest. Hoy and Miskel focused on the school system as a systems organization. They identified four key elements that affect school as a systems organization, including structure, the individual, culture and climate, and power and politics. Hoy and Miskel argued that these four elements have to function together as a whole in order for the organization to attain their mission and vision. The purpose of this sub-section is to describe these four elements in relation to schools as a social system. In addition, this section will examine how these four elements assist in improving, directing, and shaping the process of teaching and learning in a K-12 learning environment.

Structure

The word structure could refer to the physical properties of a building. The structure might include the size, shape, and materials used in constructing the building that houses an organization. However, Hoy and Miskel (1978) described structure as the daily, quarterly, and yearly routines that are in place to effectively and sometimes destructively run an organization such as a school system. Hoy and Miskel claimed that structures in the school system include the demands, duties, and responsibilities that the organization desires of its members or staff. Hoy and Miskel defined these duties and responsibilities as "bureaucratic roles" (p.25), and they noted that these roles include expectations, which are turned into specific positions in the organization. Hoy and Miskel also noted that these bureaucratic roles help determine the most appropriate behavior, conduct, and performance for a particular position. For example, a teacher is required to design lesson plans and teaching strategies that are most beneficial for student achievement. The principal has the obligation to provide instructional support and materials for teachers so that they can improve student learning. Thus, bureaucratic roles are the design for action that an organization instills in a specific position.

In addition, Hoy and Miskel (1978) noted that some of these formal demands and obligations are important and compulsory; others are more flexible. They reported that many of these formal duties and responsibilities are not specifically defined. In other words, these duties and expectations might take different forms, depending on the needs of the organization. For instance, teachers with different backgrounds and personalities are able to work in the same role without worry or disagreement and can channel their energies to accomplish a common goal. Hoy and Miskel claimed that responsibilities are also often acquired from other responsibilities in the organization; hence, roles need to be balanced with one another. Another example, it is difficult to describe the role of a teacher and a student without describing the relationship between them. The same applies to the roles of the school administrator and the teacher; the relationship between the teacher and student or the teacher and school administrator must first be described.

Although some formal organizations describe a few simple bureaucratic expectations that actually match the organization goals and vision, Hoy and Miskel (1978) contended that these expectations are often accepted as the official modus operandi for the organization. Hoy and Miskel noted that factors such as time of arrival and departure, building assignment, dress code, and job descriptions as some of the rules that formal organization might include as duties and responsibilities in relation to specific positions. For example, school systems often include these operational procedures in teacher handbooks. Moreover, a teacher is expected to act appropriately, based on the school's rules and the demands of the profession.

Thus, Hoy and Miskel (1978) argued that formal organizations such as school systems are divided into several segments called structures.

They claimed that these structures are composed of "bureaucratic expectations and roles, a hierarchy of offices and positions, rules and regulations, and specialization" (p.25). In their description of the structures in an organization, Hoy and Miskel explained that bureaucratic expectations define organizational roles and that roles are organized into positions and offices and that positions and offices are put together into formal lines of power and leadership. They claimed that rules and regulations are used to maintain order and decision-making in the organization. However, Hoy and Miskel acknowledged that structures can assist in moving the organization forward to success, but some structures could also antagonize or hinder organizational progress.

Individual Members

Hoy and Miskel (1978) argued that in an organization, regardless of the structures that are in place, members often do not follow the rules. They noted that in spite of official expectations, individual members of an organization come with personal desires, attitudes, and cognitive understanding of their positions. For example, in a school system, teachers are often considered as leaders in the classroom and tend to work alone; thus, all instructional strategies and content deliveries are different from one teacher to the other. The reason for these differences is what Deal and Peterson (2009) referred as cultural differences that teachers bring to the school environment.

They claimed that these differences in culture drive individual desires, approaches, and cognitive understanding of job positions or titles. This example is not limited to teachers; it can relate to school administrators, student personnel staff, and others such as custodians and food services workers.

Although the structural requirements and individual needs, beliefs, and cognitive understanding of the job might be in place, Hoy and Miskel (1978) argued that not all expectations and structural protocols are important when examining organizational behavior. Similarly, they noted that not all individual needs are appropriate to organizational performance. Hoy and Miskel characterized work motivation as the most prominent need of individuals in a job environment. They defined work needs as the essential force that motivates work performance.

Hoy and Miskel (1978) also argued that cognition is the mental representation that individuals assign to their jobs in relation to insight, knowledge, and expected conduct. They noted that individuals develop a clear understanding of job expectations and behavior regardless of its intricacies. According to Hoy and Miskel, individuals in an organization learn about their job performance by examining and scrutinizing their own conduct. In other words, Hoy and Miskel believed that individual's uses personal needs, beliefs, goals, and past experiences in developing organizational reality and in understanding their work behavior.

Hoy and Miskel (1978) argued that individual behavior in an organization is a function of the interaction between bureaucratic role expectations and the work orientation of the organizational member. In other words, individual needs in the organization influence the outcome of individual performances, including both cognitive and motivational needs. For instance, the evaluation of teachers is affected by central office protocols as well as by the principal's individual needs. The rules and regulations stipulate that the principal is expected to evaluate each teacher at given times with a specific assessment instrument. The principal carries out his or her duty based on these guiding principles. Every principal's actions differ in the evaluation meeting, because of individual cognitive and motivational needs. In this example, Hoy and Miskel asserted that each principal might approach the teacher evaluation from different directions. They argued that one principal may be lenient in order to gain social acceptance from the teachers, and the other principal may follow the book, lacking the need for social acceptance by the teachers. Thus, the first principal is influenced by personal needs, whereas the second principal is influenced by bureaucratic role expectations, which is the structure that is in place.

Hoy and Miskel (1978) believed that the ratio between bureaucratic expectations to individual job needs is different, based on the type of organization, the specific job, and the person doing the job. They concluded that there is variation in the structural expectations that an organization expects and that individual needs can affect the performance outcomes of an organization. In addition, Hoy and Miskel agreed that the interactions in various organizations are often scaled; some organizations are either in the low, middle, or high end in terms of bureaucratic expectations. For example, military organizations tend to be consistently at the high end of bureaucratic expectations; research based companies often appear at the low end of bureaucratic expectations. School systems often fall in the middle and high end of the bureaucratic expectations, depending if the school system is public, private, or parochial. According to Hoy and Miskel, public school systems fall under low bureaucratic expectation, whereas private and parochial institutions falls on the border line between middle and high bureaucratic expectations.

Culture and Climate

Hoy and Miskel (1978) noted that people come together in an organization to interact and work towards a common goal; from their association, they create norms, beliefs, ways of thinking, and shared values. These shared orientations are the basis for the development of a culture in an organization. Hoy and Miskel noted that culture is the one factor that distinguishes one organization from another and enables its members to acquire some kind of an identity. Hoy and Miskel claimed that in a school, shared values and relaxed norms among teachers have a powerful impact on their conduct. Hoy and Miskel also noted that culture gives members a strong commitment to something greater than themselves; that is, individuals interact in a group larger than themselves. In addition, they noted that when the culture of a group is strong, so are the members and their influence.

Hoy and Miskel also noted that culture is the intangible part of an organization; thus, contact among members becomes friendly and easier without being judgmental. They contended that the cohesiveness among members due to shared values and beliefs creates integrity, self-respect, and belonging. In addition, they claimed that many interactions in an organization with a strong culture are informal; therefore, these interactions are personal and are not dominated by the need to control power. According to Hoy and Miskel, these interactions allow individuals to maintain their character against bureaucratic expectation. For example, the mission and vision statement serve as a guide (mission) and goals (vision) for the school (Ramsey, 2009). Teachers and school administrators working together to develop these two documents create informal rules, rather than a select few who would create formal rules. These informal procedures allow all members in the school community to accept and buy into the content of the documents, creating a working relationship that is collegial.

Hoy and Miskel (1978) contended that where behavior in an organization is not controlled by structure and individual elements, shared orientation and values play a significant role. They pointed out that organizational culture is an important element that affects organizational behavior. For example, something as trivial as a school mascot may be such a strong cultural influence in a school that the removal of the mascot may create chaos among some students, teachers, and the community. Deal and Peterson (2009) suggested that the artifacts found in schools represent different things for different people. For instance, they reported that in schools with diverse student groups, the school mascot may be the only thing that connects some students to the school. In addition, with this mascot, the community may have a sense of ownership, and the mascot could be the only thing reminding them of the history of their school.

Power and Politics

Hoy and Miskel (1978) theorized that politics is the element that creates or converts the informal power that exists in an organization in order to combat or destabilize the legitimate establishment or the formal authority. Hoy and Miskel argued that structure provides formal authority; culture creates informal authority and individuals bring their authority to the organization. On the other hand, politics is unceremonious, typically secret, and frequently dishonest. Hoy and Miskel argued that politics is dishonest because its conduct is developed to benefit individuals or groups at the expense of the organization. As a result, most politics is disruptive and divisive, creating conflicts for individuals and groups against another and against organizations at large.

Hoy and Miskel (1978) noted that politics is an inevitable part of an organization; consequently, there are people who want to acquire power to benefit or move personal agendas at all costs. In other words, Hoy and Miskel believed that in an organization, politics could be seen as competing power, driving to influence policy and agendas. Hoy and Miskel argued that power relationships in an organization are played in different ways. They acknowledged that many individuals who are not interested in politics are often forced to play the game in order to survive or retain their jobs. Hoy and Miskel also contended that many people play the political game in an organization in order to get promoted, even to the point of sacrificing the integrity of an organization.

According to Hoy and Miskel (1978), although politics may be the element that brings chaos and instability to an organization, it is also a very strong force that influences organizational behavior. For example, a middle school principal decided to hire an assistant principal whose sexual orientation was of same sex, and the principal informed the teaching faculty about his intention to hire an administrator whose sexual preference was out of the norm. The principal's reason for this move was that he wanted to give a voice to students at this middle school whose sexual preference also did not conform to the norm. However, there was outrage when the community was informed about this hiring; the school was eventually shut down and reconstituted as another middle school with new leaders and teaching staff.

In conclusion, Hoy and Miskel (1978) claimed that in order to understand an organization, such as a school system, one must look at the formal and informal as well as genuine and illegal forms of authority. Therefore, structure, individual, culture, and politics are the most important elements of a social system. These elements can serve as a window through which to observe organizational behavior; however, one should not lose the sight that individual behavior is a function of the combination of these elements.

Wheatley's New Science
Wheatley's (1999) book titled *Leadership and the New Science: Discovering Order in a Chaotic World* focused on the premise that the directions provided by new theories in science are very important in managing the issues found in organizations. Wheatley contended that for an organization to thrive and succeed, it has to embrace entirely new ways of organizing. Wheatley noted that the new ways of organizing could be clearly identified in the new theories of science. The type of theories that Wheatley referenced are not the seventeen century discoveries of Isaac Newton and Rene Descartes that are still with the world today, but the type of scientific thinking that allows people to use

scientific knowledge, think individually, innovate, and come together as a whole. Wheatley (1999) claimed that cyberspace and electronic communication have changed how people work together, do business, and create relationships with each another. Wheatley acknowledged that the new technology has hastened the way life is lived and often produces feeling of inconsistency and estrangement in relationships. Wheatley argued that the new technologies are not the issue. The issue is that individuals and their organizations are still using the scientific ideas of the seventeenth century to work with new discoveries in today's society.

Simpler Ways to Lead Organizations

Wheatley (1999) argued that new ways of thinking about the work individuals do sustain-productivity, order, and ability. According to Wheatley, the new sciences are the tools to accomplish the vision mentioned earlier. She claimed that the new sciences allow individuals to observe creative and dynamic processes, nonstop change, and the innate orderliness of the universe. Wheatley argued that the innate orderliness of the universe is a clear example of a simpler way to lead an organization, a process that needs less effort and generates less stress than what is currently put into practice in many organizations.

Wheatley (1999) also believed that organizations are not unmanageable in an unpredictable ever changing world; rather the current ways of organizing are obsolete. She contended that the longer organizations remain in their old ways, the easier it is for the group to miss the exciting breakthroughs generated by the new sciences. For example, in school systems, the principal could be effective if he or she employs democratic governance for the school (Ramsey, 2009). In this process, he or she could seek ideas from teachers and staff before making decision for the entire school. The same democratic governance applies to district superintendent, school board, and teachers' unions, too.

Wheatley also commented that levels of complexity are signs of individual failure to understand the inner reality organizational life and perhaps life itself. For example, the use of cell phones is one of the new technologies that have changed society, including schools. Students and teachers are constantly using cell phones from text messaging to making quick calls. Despite the change, school systems are still using the factory model to instruct students. Cell phone use has become a big distraction for classrooms when used inappropriately. Schools have failed to incorporate cell phone use as part of the curriculum; rather, cell phone use has become punitive and an issue of conflict between teachers and students. According to Wheatley, new technologies need to be considered as another teaching tool. The factory model of education is obsolete and has no business in today's school system. Society has moved on, and schools need to move on as well (Hunter,

1994). Examples of the use of new technologies outside the school system are the telephone and the Internet, which are available to patients in the ordering of prescription drugs. With this drug ordering process, doctors can send a drug order directly to the pharmacy, rather than sending a paper prescription that needs to be delivered in person.

Wheatley (1999) also argued that accepting the nature of things and then asking the right questions in times of confusion will assist individuals in avoiding disagreements. Wheatley used the story of Bohr and Heisenburg, two founders of quantum theory in physics, as an example. Wheatley explained how the works of these physicists in relation to atomic theory led them to many questions in order to understand the universe. Wheatley reported that each time Bohr and Heisenberg came close to a solution; nature threw in a contradiction that required more questions. Wheatley claimed that the quest become successful when the two physicists started asking the right questions, which led to fewer contradictions and to their success in generating quantum theory. Wheatley believed that others could learn from the process which Bohr and Heisenburg used to tackle the problem of how the universe works and apply it in solving problems that affect organizations.

Wheatley (1999) argued that solutions to problems that worked in the past will not be appropriate for today's society. For example, in the past, students who chewed gum in the classroom during a lecture were a big distraction. Today, teachers are not worried about students who chew gum; the biggest concern is text messaging and cell phone use among adolescents. Consequently, Wheatley argued that problems change with time; therefore, problems need to be resolved by examining them from alternative perspectives. Wheatley contended that in order to use conscience effectively, one has to muster courage to let go of the old ways, to give up what individuals accept as the norm and to abandon the majority of explanations about what works and what does not work. Wheatley believes that people need to see the world as new, nothing more or less.

Wheatley (1999) also contended that members in an organization are the resources who make things work. Wheatley comments that organizations need to look at its members as resources and tap into their creativity. She contended that the new physics explains that there is no other reality outside the organization waiting to reveal its secrets. Wheatley argued that if circumstances, situations, and frameworks are as important as the science elucidates, then nothing is actually conveyed; everything is constantly new and different to individuals. Wheatley argued that individuals must connect with one another, investigate to see what works for all, and support one another as the true architects that humans are.

Similarly, Wheatley (1999) characterized the quantum worldview as the key to understanding the reality of world phenomenon. She claimed that relationships are the solution for every problem. For example, Wheatley described the relationships formed between subatomic particles as part of the process to create the atom. Wheatley noted that the same relationship could be used in an organization, where individuals still maintain autonomy yet are a part of the whole. Her thinking leads to new relations of occurrence that cannot be condensed to effortless cause and effect or explicated by examining the parts of a remote contributor. According to Wheatley, to a certain extent, individuals proceed to the point that it becomes important to sense the workings of active processes and to notice how these processes become visible actions and structures.

In order to further delineate the machine model of life with the dynamics of living systems, Wheatley (1999) highlighted examples from biology and human health as a whole system, yet functioning independently. In biology, Wheatley acknowledged that non-mechanical models of life are replaced with more holistic, active ones. For example, this replacement is done in the study of the food chain in ecology; according to Wheatley, individuals or living things in the food chain need to be studied as a whole rather than as a single entity. Wheatley argued that the focus should be on the relationships that relate individuals to the whole. In human health, for example, Wheatley claimed that the body is seen as integrated system instead of separate parts. Wheatley noted that some biologists agree that systems such as immunology, endocrinology, and neurology are better understood as one system, independently functioning on their own. In essence, Wheatley believed that as humans abandon the machine model of life and embrace the dynamics of living systems, individuals begin to learn and understand fluctuations, disorders, and change.

Wheatley (1999) also discussed the new understandings of change and disorder that have emerged from chaos theory. In chaos theory, Wheatley contended that chaos is the process that leads to a new innovative order. She noted that change that leads to order in an organization will not occur until some kind of chaos sweeps through the organization. Wheatley observed that chaos and order are mirror images, two positions that restrain the other. Wheatley noted that chaos and order are systems that can descend into one or the other, yet within either of the states, the system is held within limits that are predictable. Wheatley believed that without the partnership that exists between chaos and order, no change or progress is possible. Furthermore, Wheatley claimed that humans are very much aware of the partnership that exists between chaos and order in most cultures and that individuals need science to remind them of this partnership.

Wheatley (1999) reported that new science is helping humans to be aware that autonomy and broadmindedness are the crucial factors that all living things share. Wheatley contended that scientists describe how order and form are developed, or designed, not by complex controls but by a few guiding principles repeating themselves through the existence of individual liberty. Wheatley argued that systems such as large ecosystems to the smallest microbial colonies are maintained by simple principles that show the system identity in combination with strong levels of independency for individuals or creatures inside the system.

Wheatley (1999) also believed that the world described by the new science is changing human attitudes and insights in different areas, not only in the sciences. She noted that the new science has gradually crept into various disciplines. For example, problems in school leadership are being examined for its relationship characteristics. According to Wheatley, the intricacy of relationships that add to a leader's effectiveness can no longer be ignored. Wheatley also acknowledged that more investigations are needed in relation to partnerships, followership, empowerment, teams, networks, and the role of the environment.

Change, Stability, and Renewal

Wheatley (1999) believed that humans are recognizing that organizations are complete systems and are developing, maintaining, and sustaining them as living and learning systems. She claimed that most issues that affect an organization, such as change, chaos, surplus information, and well-established behaviors, will disappear or be reduced if humans accept the fact that organizations are living systems, with the capability for growth and adaptation, which is also common to all life processes. In addition, Wheatley argued that the human concept of organization in today's society is moving away from the machine model that thrived during the age of bureaucracy. Wheatley insisted that humans are embracing organizational structures that hold no boundaries and are flawless by default.

Consequently, Wheatley (1999) pointed out that the last destination in the universe is death; therefore, humans live in fear of change. According to Wheatley, the idea of change, no matter how insignificant, brings individuals mind closer to the end of time. Change is an unsubstantiated fear that drains valuable energy and resources which could be re-directed to other things in life, such as building effective relationships that keep group ambitions, mission, and schemes together. Change is inevitable (Deal & Peterson, 2009), and to refuse to change means to defend the wearing away of the forces of the natural world. Wheatley noted that individuals will fight change because the only destination that awaits them is death; therefore, any form of no apparent change is preferable to the known future of the end of time.

On the other hand, Wheatley (1999) claimed, in the process of trying to create equilibrium, humans have eliminated factors, which contribute to the important processes that

217

promote life. Wheatley notes that humans treat organizations like piece of equipments, acting as if they were deceased; however, organizations are living systems that are capable of evolving. Individuals have enlarged this calamity by treating one another as inanimate objects. As Wheatley noted, "Humans are believing the only way we could motivate others was by pushing and prodding them into action, overcoming their inertia by sheer force of our own energy" (p. 77). Many unanswered questions still linger: Can humans respond to life as it is without the deathwatch? Can humans leave things in their original form, attempting to keep things in balance, yet stay open to the imminent part of change?

In order to answer these questions, Wheatley introduced two concepts from the biological sciences, negative feedback and positive feedback. According to Marieb (2003), negative feedback is a loop or circular process that the human body uses to maintain internal stability and the well being of the human body, a function called homeostasis. Positive feedback is a one-time process that allows the body to go through instant, one-time change. For example, the delivery of a newborn baby is an example of positive feedback, whereas the removal and addition of calcium in the blood and in the bones by the hormones (Calcitonin and parathyroid hormone) is an example of negative feedback. Wheatley argued that the same systems that maintain stability in the human body could be emulated in organizations in order to keep organizations functioning effectively. Wheatley noted that negative feedback could be a regulatory process used to maintain a signal's deviations from established norms. In addition, Wheatley reported that positive feedback could serve as the change force that affects an organization and its members in relation to growth and accomplishment. Wheatley contended that positive feedback is not regulatory in nature, but is used to notice something new and tends to increase the signal for an organization's need for a change. Negative feedback is used to maintain and keep the system on track once the path of the organization has been established, probably by positive feedback.

In conclusion, Wheatley (1999) focused on new ways and ideas to see change as a force that allow open systems such as the educational environment to reach and maintain equilibrium. She commented that

> We are all pioneers and discoverers of a new world, and we all need one another. It is up to us to journey forth in search of new practices and new ideas that will enable us to create lives and organizations worthy of human habitation (p. xi).

Wheatley emphasized the need to discover new ways to work together for a common goal. She acknowledged that the old ways of building relationships with each other do not support human endeavors any more, whether it is at home, in the community, at work, or as a nation. Wheatley encouraged members of any organization to accept new challenges and work for the whole, yet still maintain autonomy.

Comparison and Contrast of the Theories

In his theory of the learning organization, Senge (2006) mainly focused on business environments; however, he believes that school systems also need to be organized as learning communities. Senge argued that the success of an organization comes from the members of the organization who are constantly learning. Hoy and Miskel (1978) shared the same ideas with Senge. However, the difference is that Hoy and Miskel (1978) focused on the elements that create and sustain leadership in the school community, while Senge focused on organizing and managing successful corporations. Wheatley (1999) seemed to relate to Senge's theory of the learning organization, but with slight changes. Wheatley believes that beyond the constant learning of an organization, the corporation or the school system needs to be seen as a living system capable of evolving, growing, and adaptations. Wheatley and Senge do not specifically mention educational systems in their discussion about learning organizations and corporate change, unlike Hoy and Miskel.

Wheatley (1999) argued that current ways of doing business in organizations are obsolete. She insisted that to create and sustain an effective system, individuals should look to the new sciences for assistance. In addition,

Wheatley argued that organizations should not be treated as a piece of equipment that can be used and tossed away, but as a living organism living on its own. Wheatley considered the old ways of solving problems and organizing as a machine model. Thus, she argued that every part of an organization should be seen as a living open system that is capable of evolving. Wheatley believed that this conception is the only way that individuals in the system will innovate for the greater good of the organization. Wheatley argued that chaos and disorder are legitimate parts of an organization. In this regard, she acknowledged that chaos and disorder are an early process that organizations need to pass through in order to maintain equilibrium.

Similarly, Hoy and Miskel (1978) agreed about the presence of chaos and disorder in an organization; however, they did not agree that chaos and disorder should be allowed to run its course in an organization. Hoy and Miskel contended that some controls need to be in place or incorporated into the organization to prevent or limit the damage caused by chaos and disorder. Hoy and Miskel also believed that elements such as structure, individuals, culture and climate, and power and politics are strong organizational tools that assist organizations in maintaining order. Hoy and Miskel pointed out that the same elements can also destroy organizations if they are not properly used.

In contrast, Senge (2006) did not specifically describe the presence of chaos and disorder in learning organizations. Rather, he argued, although the individual in an organization works and thinks independently, he or she needs to act as part of a whole for the benefit and survival of the organization. In order to support this behavior, Senge encouraged members of the organization to avoid generalizations, assumptions, and mental images that are not clarified. Furthermore, Senge noted, to avoid conflict and share mutual trust among individuals in an organization, one has to learn to lift images and assumptions from the subconscious level and make them part of the conscious level. Wheatley (1999) added that in order to sustain effective relationships and to develop collegiality among staff members, individuals must let go of their old ways of thinking and embrace new ways of thinking with the changes that follows.

School systems across the United States are under extreme pressure to raise test scores within the instructional system, K-12. Increasing the feedback from teachers, students, and the community helps to specify the functions of the systems. The specification of an outcome is an important trait of systems theory in education today (Hoy & Miskel, 1978). However, sometimes educators, policy makers, and the community mistake systems approaches as a way to control or hold back teachers' instructional expertise in a classroom. Systems thinking can be the principal architect in changing the low productivity and academic achievement of students. Educational systems must look beyond traditional structures and create learning organizations that work. Students in the educational system today are not performing as well as they should. Some underlining reasons for this lack of progress could be credited to a lack of effective planning on the part of educators. Current studies in the next section will indicate that teachers as reflective instructional practitioners play an important part in teaching and learning, specifically in inner-city schools. Teachers need to use instructional strategies that allow students to transfer knowledge and improve retention so that academic achievement can be improved for all students. The k-12 system needs to improve student transfer of knowledge, retention, and student achievement in general. In section VI, the literature will be reviewed in relation to accountability, achievement, performance, and school organizing structures as a means to enhance student achievement.

SECTION VI

Science Literacy...Strategies of Instruction

In order to meet the needs of the new century society and live comfortably in a fast growing technological society, students need not only be trained in the area of science, but understand the fundamental knowledge of science literacy (Palmer, 2008). Scientific literacy involves learning about the Nature of Science (NOS) and scientific concepts. According to a study by Lotter, Singer, and Godlley (2009), people should be able to use scientific knowledge to make informed decisions that will benefit them and the larger society.

Furthermore, science education as the means to creating a user friendly technological future encourages individuals, community members, educators, and education policy makers to pay attention to science education in high schools across America. Sampson and Gerbino (2010) contended that students need to learn and understand how scientific theories, concepts, and laws are generated. This task is a process that teachers are charged to accomplish; however, the task is not that simple to accomplish, considering the present design of science classrooms in the public schools. Sampson and Gerbino argued that the task of improving science education could yield few results unless specific instructional strategies or techniques are available to teachers as a template for science instruction. For example,

Sampson and Gerbino designed exemplary instructional strategies known as the "generate-an-argument" model and the "evaluate alternatives" model. In these two models, they described a protocol that allows students to work closely with one another in discovering scientific claims. This protocol reduces the amount of time a science teacher needs to spend providing direct instruction on the topic and encourages the teacher to serve as a facilitator of the instruction.

On the other hand, Lotter, Singer, and Godlley (2009) argued that using a variety of instructional techniques is possible; however, teachers need to organize the framework of teaching to accord time to repeat, reflect, and re-teach in order for the instructional strategies to be effective. Gioka (2009) found that instructional strategies in science focus on teaching for assessment. Gioka recommended that teachers pay more attention to the instructional strategies in science that allow students to discover where they are in their learning, where they might go, and how to proceed.

In essence, the instructional strategies employed in a classroom will depend on the worldview of the instructor. Researchers have indicated that many instructional techniques (Cook, 2009; Sampson & Gerbino, 2010; Sorgo, 2010, Stephens & Winterbottom, 2010) employed by teachers in science classes are often related to performance based learning (PBL), inquiry, and collaborative learning. These strategies tend to create academic deficiencies or challenges for some groups of students (Gredler, 2009).

Although empirical studies indicate the benefit of constructivist and inquiry-based instruction in science, especially in biology courses, other researchers (Waters & Waters, 2007; Gredler, 2009; Love, 2010) argued against using inquiry-based learning as the only teaching method. These researchers reported that a worldview such as constructivism is inappropriate for low ability learners and students from different cultures. Using constructivism as the foundation for instruction often increases the workload of the teacher in relation to lesson plans and preparation time. These researchers also argued that teachers using this approach do not ask challenging questions. Additionally, recent research has revealed that the absence of guided instruction or lecture-based instruction negatively impacts the learning of students (Mualem & Eylon, 2006; Caravita, Valente, Pace, Valanides, Khalil, Berthou, Kozan-Naumescu, & Clement, 2008)

The purpose of this section is to describe research literature in relation to instructional strategies that are used in science education, particularly in biology at the high school level. This section will also describe instructional strategies that are related to student motivation to learn, student retention, transfer of knowledge, and the impact of student diversity on teacher lesson design in high school biology courses.

Instructional Framework

An instructional framework should provide teachers with a valuable instructional tool that leads to a high level of student engagement and learning. This instructional framework is often based on beliefs related to constructivism and differentiated instruction (Tomilinson, 2004; Gredler, 2009). Effective instruction in science includes (a) discovering what students know and are able to do, (b) what they have learned, and (c) what intervention is needed (Waters & Watters, 2007). Teachers know what to teach, based on the national, state, and district science education standards. Teachers use specific instructional tools to improve teaching and ensure that the objective of the lesson has been met (Hunter, 2004; Hunt, Wiseman, & Touzel, 2009; Marzano, Pickering, & Pollock, 2001). After each lesson, the teacher will assess what each child has learned. Where is each student on the learning continuum? Teachers use the records from their assessments to determine which students have mastered the science concepts and which students still need assistance. This assessment information needs to drive science instruction (Hunter, 2004). When students who need further assistance have been identified, teachers must select suitable instructional intervention strategies to ensure student success. Teachers need to alter lessons as needed and eventually start the process again. The framework presented below organizes best practice in relation to the following three factors: (a) determine the intended learning, (b) design the learning process, and (c) attend to student work (Sorgo, 2010).

Determine the Intended Learning. At the beginning of each lesson, teachers need to state the content and evidence of the lesson, which they plan to teach for the class period. The statement of content and evidence could be a title or a question that relates to the topic of the lesson. The topic or title of the lesson could also serve as an evidence of the material to be learned by the students. Starting instruction with a title or a question in mind will drive the instruction (Campbell, Oh, Shin, & Zhang, 2010). The title of a lesson also allows students to imagine what the lesson is all about, and it is what Love (2010) described as the key to awakening student imagination.

After the title or the question has been explicitly displayed, the teacher needs to state the objective of the lesson (Student Learning Objectives-SLO). This objective must specify what students will learn and be able to do at the end of the instruction or teaching activity. The objective could be questions or statements that articulate what the student will grasp at the end of the teaching period. The objectives need to be also displayed for students to see and anticipate where the teacher is going with the instruction. Many researchers have argued that teachers need to encourage students to generate objectives of their own based on the written objectives of the lesson (Caravita, Valente, Luzi, Pace, Valanides, Khalil, & Clément, 2008;

228

Hunter, 2004; Wong & Day, 2009). At the end of the lesson, teachers and students should examine both objectives in order to see if the intended learning was achieved.

However, before the teacher states the content, evidence, and the objectives of the lesson, he or she must determine the level of difficulty of the lesson proposed. At this point, the teacher should have a fairly good understanding of the students' abilities, motivations, and readiness for the challenges of instruction. Based on this knowledge of the students' capabilities, the teacher can then set the level of difficulty for the instruction.

Monitoring students' completed assignments can do the teacher setting the level of difficulty for the lesson. Lesson plans can be adjusted based on how well the students' work shows mastery of instruction. Teachers can move instruction up and down a scale set by the teacher (Watters & Watters, 2007) during a teaching unit. According to Watters and Watters, teachers at some point during the instruction have to make a judgment call to adjust instruction. If many of the students are not learning the lesson as prescribed, the teacher needs to adjust the lesson downwards. Some teachers oppose the idea of adjusting instruction at the expense of high level performing students (Campbell, Oh, Shin, & Zhang, 2010; Sorgo, 2010; Wong & Day, 2009). These researchers recommend differentiating instruction in the class and allowing struggling students and high performing students to learn at their pace, without losing instructional time at both ends.

Empirical studies have revealed that in many classrooms determining the intended learning of the instruction relates to information given to the students as well as the activities completed by the students and the questions that are asked and the responses given to the questions during the lesson (Cook, 2009; Sampson & Gerbino, 2010). For each lesson, the intended learning is the outcome; therefore, teachers need to be purposeful about the type of information that they present to students during the lesson. In addition, activities that justify the intended learning must be carefully planned in order to help students master what they should learn and be able to do at the end of the lesson. Also, the questions teachers ask during instruction must be carefully selected or designed to stimulate student cognition, which will lead to the intended goal. Cook argued if questions are generated correctly and purposefully with the lesson objective in mind, excellent learning responses will be elicited from the students.

Design the Lesson. In order to design an effective lesson, the teacher has to relate to students in terms of how they acquire knowledge by the use of reasoning, intuition, or perception. The teacher needs to probe the cognitive tools before selecting a particular instructional strategy to deliver the lesson. The next logical step for the teacher is to plan a lesson based on this information. During pre-teaching and post teaching, the teacher must assume responsibility for the learning that transpires in his or her classroom. For example, if a well planned lesson does not go very well and the majority of students are still lost in relation to mastering the outcomes of the lesson, it is the responsibility of the teacher to re-teach the lesson, preferably with a different instructional strategy that meets the needs of all students (Cook, 2010; Wong & Day, 2009; Watters & Watters, 2007; Hunter, 2004).

Attend to Student Needs. Today's classroom is much more diverse than ever before. Not too long ago, the Civil Rights movement and the First Amendment found in the United States Constitution have indirectly accorded individuals the right to seek a basic education (Deal & Peterson, 2009). With these rights, teachers need to consider the learning styles of students, the gender of the student, the cultural background or ethnicity of the students, and their natural abilities in relation to academic learning. In other words, teachers in science education need to consider several factors about their students before designing a lesson, including the attitudes and behaviors observed in group dynamics, especially in relation to gender stereotypes and family values in comparison with those of the teachers or the mainstream student population. For example, many science teachers tend to recognize male students more often than female students during class activities or interactions. Childs and McNichol (2007) claimed that such behavior is common in science and mathematics classes. This typical gender stereotype among teachers sometimes is not intentional; however, teachers need to be conscious of such behavior when interacting with students. In addition, Childs and McNichol recommended that teachers include sensitivity to gender issue in planning science lessons.

The impact of cultural background or ethnicity on student learning needs in the classroom also needs to be considered. Deal and Peterson (2009) reported that the diversity of student in today's classroom have created the need for teachers to pay attention to the values that students bring to the classroom and to the school. For example, the teaching of evolutionary theory in biology classes in high schools is often an issue today. Many families have strong religious beliefs, especially Christian families who have strong reservations about allowing their children to learn about evolutionary theory as developed by Charles Darwin. Cook (2009) suggested that biology teachers create situations in the classroom that encourage students to expose their current and prior beliefs about evolution and examine and contrast those beliefs with current scientific views. Furthermore, some researchers (Anderson, 2007; Cook, 2009) have recommended that biology teachers explicitly link the teaching of evolutionary theory to the teaching of the nature of science in an effort to increase student skills in interpreting such theories as specified in the national science education standards.

Supporting internal and external motivation during instruction will also generate avenues to attend to student learning needs. One area of concern is what Hunter (2004) called feeling tone. The teacher needs to act in a professional manner when speaking or conferencing with students and their family. Students watch attitudes and behaviors exhibited by teachers and are often critical of such attitudes and behaviors (Ramsey, 2009). Thus, teachers must be careful about how to approach a conference with students and their parents. Language should be empathic in nature, and teachers should not comment on issues that have nothing to do with teaching and learning (Deal & Peterson, 2009).

Marieb (2003) noted that the hormones of teenage students are responsible for the majority of their behavior. Teachers in science classrooms need to act accordingly to avoid issues that will create a lack of sensitivity and not allow them to meet the learning needs of the students. Sympathy on the part of teachers will lead to internal motivation on the part of students. For example, a sympathetic attitude model by the teacher (Deal & Peterson, 2009; Ramsey, 2009) will allow students to imitate such an attitude and increase their external motivation.

Intended Learning and Knowledge Acquisition in Biology

The best time to specify intended learning in biological science is at the beginning of the class before the objectives are presented and after the subject is introduced. For example, in a biology lesson, the goal may be for students to master words associated with the work of Gregory Mendel in genetics. The goal of the lesson can also be classified as intended learning. For a science lesson the intended goal is stated early, after the main topic or title of the subject. One of the reasons for stating the intended learning early is to allow students to think about what need to be accomplished in the lesson (Marzano, Pickering, & Pollock, 2001) and to re-kindle their imagination. In addition, stating the intended learning early in a biology lesson assists the teacher and students in focusing on specific science concepts rather than general concepts. In other words, stating the intended learning will help teacher stay on target without confusing students.

When students know that they have acquired the knowledge, skills, and attitudes of a lesson, they will be less disruptive, more engaged in the class activity, and complete assigned work independently (Cook, 2009). For example, when generating a specific lesson plan in science using specific vocabulary words such as *splash*, the teacher may ask students to rearrange the words based on their understanding of the terms. The vocabulary words: can be arranged by comparing and contrasting them, classifying them, or placing them into categories that are familiar to students. The teacher should allow students to work together, moving words around and classifying them. The teacher acts as a facilitator, focusing on the independence that students exhibit while completing the activity. In addition, the teacher observes the feeling tone of students during the activity in relation to the level of difficulty. At this point, it is assumed that the teacher has established an atmosphere in the science classroom that allows students to want to learn and succeed. For example, as the teacher is walking around the classroom working with students, he or she might choose to encourage students using pleasant words (i.e. *I like the way you use those science words. It shows that you have actually mastered the subject...excellent work*). This type of pleasant language, Wong and Day (2009) explained, encourages students to work harder and want to be in the science class.

In setting the correct level of difficulty and/or monitoring and adjusting the biology lesson plan, the teacher focuses on the clarity of the lesson goals or objectives or outcomes, establishing strategies and how to monitor them (Cook, 2009; Campbell, Oh, Shin, & Zhang, 2010). For example, in a lesson plan, the goal may be for students to investigate words associated with the study of genetics and the early work of Gregory Mendel on principles of inheritance. The strategy of classification is used to deliver the lesson. In order to monitor and adjust instruction, the teacher assigns questions to each group and times the groups to see which group will respond with the correct answer in the quickest amount of time. Depending on how strong the responses are, the teacher could re-teach, move-on, or abandon the topic.

Another example of what the teacher could do with this lesson is to ask students to think about the following: "Compare and contrast gene, traits, and allele." The teacher needs to give students enough time to respond to this statement. This wait time on the part of the teacher assists students who are struggling to respond (Hochberg & Gabric, 2010). In addition, the teacher could help students by giving them the questions with the correct answers (Winterbottom & Stephens, 2010). The teacher could then ask students to use those answers to generate different answers or explanations to the questions. The teacher could also give prompts that will help students think more clearly and process the information in the lesson more clearly. For example, at the beginning of instruction, teachers could display the objectives for the lesson and ask students to generate their own objectives based on what they want to learn from the lesson.

Finally, in monitoring student progress, the teacher will obtain evidence of student success on various outcomes. The result of criterion-referenced tests could be used in evaluating the completed lesson as well as to monitor student progress. Another way of monitoring student progress is using an informal assessment known as a formative assessment (Gioka, 2009). In this type of assessment, the teacher ends the lesson by allowing students to recap or summarize the lesson. In addition, the teacher could include all students in this task by asking students to describe what they have learned, what needs to be clarified, and what they really want to know from the lesson. In essence, this strategy will show the teacher where the students are in the learning of the lesson, so that he or she will make a judgment call whether to continue instruction or to re-teach the entire lesson.

Instructional Strategies in Biology

A better way to encourage learning and student independence in learning is to create learning awareness and to make it explicit (Stephen & Winterbottom, 2010). Making learners understanding apparent to them and involving learners in active participation of the learning process will increase knowledge and retention in science education. Researchers have found that teachers feel more effective if they are able to use previously designed instructional strategies in the form of a template as a part of their lesson plan (Cook, 2009; Love, 2010). However, empirical studies have shown templates on instructional strategies are available on biology lessons for high school classes. Finding the right strategy for instructional delivery in biology depends on the amount of time the teacher is willing to spend planning for a lesson. In each lesson plan, the teacher needs to consider other issues that affect the class, such as student behavior and lack of motivation (Hunter, 2004). For example, teachers can start with vocabulary words in biology and allow students to explore a concept using prior knowledge. The teacher follows the use of that strategy with discussions clarifying misconceptions generated by students.

Another effective instructional strategy that can be used in biology is the use of a concept map (Love, 2010; Wong & Day, 2009). A concept map is a graphical representation of the biology concept materials that are taught (Love, 2010). In this case, Love argued that teachers might use concept maps to explain biological information in a more visual learning style. Such a technique allows educational modifications for students who are visual learners. The concept map used in biology instruction helps students to make connections between concepts and words in a lesson. Concept maps are connections that show how biological words link with others, and they assist students in creating mental pictures of scientific words and their application, which is a shorter version of taking notes in class.

Another strategy for biology instruction is generating questions (Stephens & Winterbottom, 2010). In this instructional strategy, the teacher generates all possible questions involving the topic to be learned. The teacher then interacts with students, asking questions and recording student responses to the questions. According to Stephens and Winterbottom, the teacher pays special attention to misconceptions and knowledge gaps among students and re-directs students when needed.

Other instructional strategies that can be used in biology are based on the work of Sampson and Gerbino (2010). They developed two strategies for science instruction known as the "generate-an-argument" strategy and the "evaluate alternatives" strategy. For example, in the "generate-an-argument strategy", students are instructed to design and complete a poster board. First, students are divided into groups, and they collect questions from the instructor for the arguments. On the poster board, students include the group's tentative claim, with the evidence and reasoning they are using to support it (i.e. their argument) as well as the goal of the investigation. Once each group has created a visual representation of their argument, the students are directed to share their findings using a round-robin presentation structure. According to Sampson and Gerbino, in a round robin structure, each group selects one person to stay with their group poster and to present their argument while the other group members rotate to each of the other groups to learn about the other arguments. Throughout this stage, students must communicate their ideas, evaluate information, and articulate any questions they may have. The ability to question or critique an argument is a valuable skill for students to develop and helps to foster important habits of mind such as skepticism and valuing evidence. This stage also helps students understand that the goal of scientific argumentation is not to win at all costs but to develop a better understanding of the phenomenon under investigation (National Research Council, 1996). It is important that the teacher allow the students enough time to discuss their arguments in details in order to maintain their focus on the topic. After students have had the opportunity to view and discuss the claims and arguments that their peers have developed, they should reconvene in their original groups to discuss their own argument again. Sampson and Gerbino noted that, at this point, students should be directed to evaluate their claims in light of all the evidence, rationales, and other claims that they have seen. If possible, the teacher should direct the students' attention to the criteria needed to establish a sufficient claim and to evaluate how well the evidence and rationales are connected to the claim.

Sampson and Gerbino (2010) also proposed that students should be prompted to fully evaluate the persuasive nature of their own arguments as well as those of the other groups. The teacher should wrap up the discussion by making explicit connections between the activity and the main concept of the lesson in order to help students understand and learn. For example, if students are learning about the circulation of human blood (Marieb, 2003), the teacher reiterates an argument concerning the circulation of human blood. Students are given an opportunity to articulate what they know and how they know it by designing their own written argument about the circulation of human blood. The teacher also needs to develop criteria and rubrics to guide students through the assignment (Gredler, 2009). The criteria and rubrics are of particular importance if the assignment involves writing.

Although the research literature indicates that these instructional strategies are effective in delivering the lesson, the concern that needs to be answered is whether these strategies meet the needs of all students of different abilities and backgrounds. For example, how do the strategies accommodate students who are English as Second Language (ESL) learners? One instructional strategy that can be used is to check student learning styles or processes when activating prior knowledge about the subject (Marzano, Pickering, & Pollock, 2001; Thompson, 2009; Gredler, 2009). Creating pre-class work or assignments before the delivery of the lesson can also activate prior knowledge. For example, the teacher can generate words associated with a lesson, providing the information to students ahead of time. Hopefully, students will complete this pre-class assignment. When the class starts, students will be asked to discuss their pre-class assignment in groups. Teachers need to encourage students to ask questions from the pre-class assignment that are not clear during the teacher lecture. At the end of the group work, students will use the criteria and rubrics developed in class to complete the assignment.

In addition, in order to check whether the instructional strategies accommodate students' learning needs, the teacher needs to pay special attention to students with academic modifications (504) or other students in the class who are struggling with the lesson. Every time the teacher attends to a specific group, he or she should ask a clarification question. For example, the teacher may ask, "How do you know that those words belong to that category?" or "What is your evidence to the claim?" or "What is your rationale behind the claim?" The teacher waits for the student to respond or will sometimes call on the students who have an accommodation to respond. If students successfully respond to each question, then the teacher feels comfortable those students are on track and that they are actually learning.

Although the class activity takes most of the teaching time, the teacher should make sure he or she focuses on the intended learning goal (Cook, 2009; Wong & Day, 2009). The teacher will be able to focus on the intended learning by implicitly reminding himself or herself of the intended learning goals and directing all comments to accomplishing the goal. For student questions that fall outside the intended learning, the teacher needs to tell students that those questions will be documented and be re-visited in the future. For example, the teacher can place a poster on one side of the classroom with markers and ask students to place those questions on the poster. The teacher could name the poster *"The Parking Lot"*.

Student Motivation

This sub-section of the paper indicates that student motivation is an area of great concern in relation to teaching and learning. Many inner city school students often experience phobias or fears about science and math, and these fears affect their test scores in science and decrease their achievement in these subjects. In addition, many researchers (McNicholl &Childs, 2007; Mualem & Eylon, 2009) reported that the reason why students develop phobias and avoid science and mathematics is because many teachers also have phobias about science and mathematics. These researchers (McNicholl &Childs, 2007; Mualem & Eylon, 2009) argued that in a school community, all teachers contribute to the teaching of English language arts. However, instruction in science and mathematics are left only to science and mathematics teachers; thus, re-enforcement of instruction in these subjects is often not provided.

Hochberg and Gabric (2010) noted that collaboration between biology and mathematics often exists. However, they noted that there is a need to expand instruction in science and mathematics beyond these classrooms. They agreed with other researchers that English Language Arts (ELA) often gets more instructional time than science and mathematics. Hochberg and Gabric also noted that the majority of teachers use English language arts in the delivery of instruction and assessment for a course, and therefore, this delivery provides additional instructional time for English language arts. Hochberg and Gabric recommended that teachers, policy makers, and educational leaders change this unbalanced instructional time by offering teachers professional development that focus on the integration of science and mathematics across the curriculum.

In the process of motivating students to participate in the learning process, the teacher employs the use of linguistic and non-linguistic tools, as well as metaphors (Egan, 1997). For example, in a lesson on genetics, students generated words in relation to the word *splash,* and they organized their brainstormed words into different categories. One way to motivate the students is to allow students to compare and contrast categories. The compare and contrast technique is one of the intellectual practices that Egan (1997) emphasized as a major tool that enables students to learn better in any academic activity. Campbell, Oh, Shin & Zhang (2010) agreed that student motivation in learning biology relies on student involvement in the activity by getting firsthand knowledge, rather than being told what to do or only reading about the subject. Campbell et al. also argued in favor of creating intellectual tools that allow students to investigate the learning. This idea generates less boredom and increases motivation among students. Campbell et el. noted that learning science concepts is much more enjoyable for students if they are allowed to apply science related knowledge and inquiry skills to solve real problem in society. Caravita, Valente, Luzi, Pace, Valanides, Khalil, & Clément (2008) also favored the idea of using intellectual tools to increase student motivation in science education. They claimed that to think, talk, and act as members of a science community starts from the interactions that are generated during the early learning of science. For example, the use of metaphors or the use of compare and contrast allows students to interact socially among themselves, creating the motivation to learn.

Although student motivation is important, teacher motivation also needs to be addressed. Students in science classrooms observe behaviors exhibited by teachers daily, and they seem to learn by imitating this teacher behavior. Therefore, if a teacher is science phobic, chances are that this phobia will affect student interest in science (Hochberg & Gabric, 2010). As stated early, teachers have a tendency to develop a phobia of science, especially if their teacher training did not involve a strong background in science. This lack of training in science becomes a problem when a high school teacher is asked to teach across the content areas. For example, a history teacher often incorporates English language arts in his or her history lesson plan because his or her training involves learning the English language, including basic writing skills. However, the same history teacher may find it difficult to do the same with science or mathematics. The problem of subject phobia, especially in science and mathematics, is one of the major problems that affect student achievement (Mualem & Eylon. 2009). Thus, if teachers also lack motivation, due to burn out, subject phobia, or lack of a strong background in the subject, student learning will also be hindered (Hunter, 1994). In order to increase teacher motivation, collegiality in teaching should be encouraged, especially where teachers can observe others. In addition, professional development should focus on alternative ways of increasing teacher efficacy of the subject. Another strategy is to increase academic rigor for teachers outside their certification through strong professional development that focuses on subjects like science and mathematics.

Motivation for students tends to diminish when students find the lesson so challenging that they are unable to attempt it. Empirical studies have revealed that students tend to be motivated by their own curiosity when presented with lessons that allow them to explore the topic rather than learning through lectures (Wong & Day, 2009). Wong and Day also argued that students should be encouraged to explore the lesson through a problem-based learning approach (PBL) in contrast with a lecture based learning (LBL) approach. However, not all instruction will fair well by PBL alone; some instructions can also benefit from the LBL techniques (Gredler, 2009). Gredler argued in favor of mixing PBL and LBL instructional practices in order not to diminish the long term memory (LTM) and working memory (WM) of students. Gredler insisted that PBL works

246

effectively for WK, but LBL is effective in activating LTM. Many other researchers agreed that there is a need to include a LBL approach to instruction. However, in the case of learning mastery, the teacher could create a pyramid of increasing rigor (Hunt, Wiseman, & Touzel, 2009). For example, the teacher starts increasing the level of difficulty of the subject up to a peak point, or the point where the academic challenge is at its highest, and then gradually comes back down, repeating the same process again.

Transfer of Knowledge

The instructional strategies that are considered highly effective for transfer of learning include comparing, classifying, and using metaphors and analogies (Stephens & Winterbottom, 2010). Signals that indicate that transfer of learning is taking place include student comfort with subject and strong student performance on an assessment. The key to transfer of knowledge in science education is based on instruction and assessment that needs to be re-focused on learning (Gioka, 2009). Issues in the classroom that affect transfer of learning include the teacher-student relationship and the language barrier for the student. A student's personal life could also be a hindrance to transfer of learning; an example could be divorce in the family (Hunter, 2004). In addition, teacher values, beliefs, worldviews, and attitudes may affect how students acquire knowledge in biology (Caravita, Valente, Luzi,

Pace, Valanides, Khalil, & Clément, 2010). These researchers claimed that the values and beliefs of teachers might be different from those of the students and their families. Thus, there may be constant conflict in the transfer of knowledge. For example, the teaching of evolution in biology does awaken some spiritual conflict between students who come from strong Christian homes and the biology teacher. In order to positively affect students' transfer of knowledge, Cook (2009) encouraged science teachers to allow students to express their beliefs about evolution as part of the instructional lesson and create a situation where students can examine and contrast their beliefs with recent generally accepted scientific views.

The skills required to implement effective teaching and learning are very complex and are also dependent upon several modalities (Love, 2010). Regardless of the unpredictable human factor in teaching and learning, there are several ways to deliver instruction to students successfully. In order to implement effective instruction, teachers need to focus on individual students, not groups (Cook, 2010). Student humanistic and worldview needs to be examined effectively before each lesson is designed. Teacher reflection is highly recommended (Lotter, 2009). Because students come from different backgrounds and with different learning needs, teachers need to reflect on their instruction before and after each lesson. Instruction can be improved when teachers pay attention to instructional frameworks that include determining the intended learning, designing the instructional processes, and attending to student needs. In addition, understanding each student and being able to meet these individual needs could be a way to assure a future where students will have the knowledge and skills to create a just society.

Retention

In the "generate-an-argument" instructional strategy discussed earlier, student writing fosters student thinking and provides a good evaluation of student abilities. In addition, this technique tends to encourage meta-cognition and improve student retention (Sampson & Gerbino, 2010). Some of the techniques recommended in the research literature to improve retention of learning include tailoring the instruction to fit students' backgrounds, using positive language to communicate with students, using students' prior knowledge when introducing a lesson, and making instruction meaningful and personal (Sorgo, 2010). For example, in the lesson on genetics, the teacher could begin instruction by asking students to interview family members about characteristics that exist in their families. When they return to school, the teacher should give students time to share their findings. This type of an assignment that involves family learning encourages students to learn from competent adults in their lives (Campbell, Oh, Shin & Zhang, 2010). In other words, learning that involves family interactions and scientific argumentation allows for quality family time and proper retention of the subject matter.

Teachers also need to model retention protocols for students. This modeling could take place in the middle of the lesson when difficult or new material is introduced to students (Sorgo, 2008). A good example involves a lesson in biology concerning the use of a microscope, where the teacher introduces a new word such as *diameter*. There are many different strategies that teachers can use to model learning retention for students. How do teachers know what retention strategies are appropriate for each student? The only possible way to know is to use different strategies often and see which one works well with all students.

Teachers could also identify the rate and degree of learning of students by paying close attention to how many students understand the clarifying questions. Teachers also need to pay attention to the end-of-class summaries in order to engage students and modify or adjust lesson plans. For example, when student's end-of-class summaries do not reflect what was taught in the class, students are not actively engaged in class work; then the teacher could teach the same topic but with a different lesson plan. Wong and Day (2008) noted that another area of interest in relation to retention is the teacher's reinforcement of learning. They also pointed out noted that performance based learning (PBL) strategy is effective in knowledge retention because PBL requires students to learn through a constructivist style; it is possible that students may have better retention of the lesson when they actively participate in an activity during the instruction.

Teachers who differentiate the assessment in an instructional lesson could also assist in knowledge retention for students (Gioka, 2009). Instead of giving the traditional test for the lesson, the teacher could use an informal assessment to monitor student progress. In a planned assessment, the teacher interprets the assessment information and responds to it. This form of assessment is carried out with the whole class. On the other hand, for interactive assessment, the teacher noticing, recognizing, and responding to students' answers and questions during lecture or an activity helps. The preceding techniques must be carried out with some individuals or groups of students.

Student Diversity and Lesson Plans in Biology

The demography of students in today's classroom has changed. Classrooms across the United States are more heterogeneous than previous years (O'Hara & Pritchard, 2008). Many of the changes have occurred in public schools, specifically in the urban community. The numbers of English as a Second Language Learners (ESL) are growing; however, teachers are not always properly trained to meet the needs of this new wave of students. With this change in the student body, teachers need to create lesson plans that meet or accommodate all backgrounds and disabilities (Marzano,

Pickering, & Pollock, 2001; Saravia-Shore and Garcia, 1992). This section of the paper will present the notion that a teacher needs to consider creating instruction that each student finds meaningful and interesting; using a multicultural teaching approach when students discuss a misconception that has a strong cultural belief in their families; and using instructional strategies that are effective and efficient with students of diverse background. The research literature indicates that teachers are encouraged to focus on the clarity of instruction. In addition, teachers need to attend to student differences covertly (O'Hara & Pritchard, 2008). For example, a typical classroom includes right and left-handed students, which means that students learn differently (Marieb, 2003). With this fact in mind, the teacher's lesson should include visuals and detailed explanations for each objective.

Lee and Buxton (2008) noted that there are many challenges in a student's family culture, values, and belief system. They argued that students in the school system already possess strong family values that shape their thinking. These values create tension for the students, because they challenge or reject lessons that diminish or reject the values of their families. In addition, Lee and Buxton insisted that this problem is common in biology classes where instruction about evolution seems to be contrary to some students' family beliefs system. In this case, the teacher needs to explain to students the differences between misconceptions and logical explanations, and at the same time being careful not to destroy their cultural and family values.

In one study, Campbell and Bohn (2008) found that the diversity in science class does not account for student performance, but rather the socio-economic status is the most significant obstacle in students' achievement in science class. Campbell and Bohn encouraged teachers to use several instructional strategies that support multicultural teaching approaches. For example, teachers can use strategies that encourage competition as stipulated by Saravia-Shore and Garcia, (1992). With this instructional technique, students are allowed to evaluate each other's work, and they are assigned grades based on the criteria developed by students. In addition, Campbell and Bohn recommended that teachers pair native English speaking students with non-native English speakers for laboratory investigations in biology.

In summary, today's biology class has changed significantly over the past few decades. These changes have been pushed by human ingenuity in such areas of investigation as cloning and the human genome project. In some school communities in the United States, these changes are driven by politics, beliefs, and values system. The academic agenda is understandable; however, the political and personal beliefs and values are the issues that need to be addressed in biology instruction at the high school level. For instance, many school districts have not developed a curricular framework for biology nor have they trained school principals and other administrators in science pedagogy and the nature of science as prescribed in the national science education standards (NRC, 1996). Therefore, it is left for the teacher to create the lessons that he or she deems appropriate for students. Biology teachers across the country are often asked to teach lessons that appear to be inappropriate to individuals who do not understand the nature of science or instructional pedagogy in biology. The lack of an agreed about the curricular framework creates significant challenge for many biology teachers who need to teach controversial topics such as evolution, sexual reproduction, and genetics. However, the literature review did not reveal any studies in this area. Yet it is important that the school principals and other administrators who supervise biology instructors become familiar with instructional pedagogy in biology.

There is no doubt the various instructional strategies explored in this paper will improve biological instruction in high schools. American students are affected by different value systems, which eventually feeds into problems related to instructional practice in biology (Caravita, Valente, Luzi, Pace, Valanides, Khalil, & Clément, 2008). In addition, the role of teachers' belief systems should not be overlooked in considering problems related to instructional delivery. However, there is no national government policy that addresses the issue of pedagogy content knowledge in biology instruction directly (Childs & McNicholl, 2007; Watters & Watters, 2007; Palmer, 2008). However, a review of the literature has revealed that there are some issues related to teachers' belief systems, such as parental education, family religion, the nature of science, and content knowledge that need to be considered in biology instruction. For example, establishing a program that could increase the awareness of school principals and education policy makers about the nature of science instruction should be considered, because this initiative could significantly improve teacher efficacy in biology instructional practice and reduce the controversy that often arises in biology instructions. In addition, ongoing professional development that creates collaboration among biology teachers and other science teachers, supervisors without science background, and school principals will benefit the system. This professional development will increase an awareness of the use of nature of science and pedagogy content knowledge in lesson design, especially in relation to lessons in biology that are controversial or that create tension for some students.

Nevertheless, instructional practices that improve student achievement science, especially in urban schools, also improve the dropout rate are valuable programs in addressing student performance in science. However, these solutions do not seem to be able to totally improve student performance in science

(Hochberg & Gabic, 2010). It is worth noting that science programs that focus on curriculum frameworks, instructional strategies, retention, and student diversity may be the most efficient way to address improvement in science achievement among high school students (Lee & Buxton, 2008; Campbel & Bohn, 2008; Lotter, Singer, & Godley, 2009; Cook, 2009; Love, 2010; Sorgo, 2010; Stephen & Winterbottom, 2010).

An exploration of the literature revealed one major issue facing science education: teachers do not use many new and innovative instructional practices that are available for teaching science and improving student learning. In addition, the literature review indicates that teachers prefer traditional teaching methods as opposed to inquiry or performance based learning, which is often time consuming. In addition, throughout this paper, much has been said about the role of teachers in improving student learning in biology. However, little was mentioned about the role of principals and other school administrators in this regard. What are the perceptions of school administrators about biological science pedagogy? The level of awareness of a school principal about biology curricula and instructional strategies calls for further research since the school principal is often considered the instructional leader in the school.

Application III

Professional Practice in Education Organization

Section V described the works of Senge, Hoy and Miskel, and Wheatley in relation to their theories about the educational organization. The work of these theorists characterized a learning organization as an institution that facilitates societal development; through such concepts as democracy, inquiry, and socially negotiated learning. Such an environment is also a vehicle for effecting positive social change (Senge, 2006; Wheately, 1999). In order to provide science teachers with guidance for using effective instructional strategies to improve achievement in science for students of different backgrounds, their theories serve as a foundation for this application section.

Section VI was an in-depth examination of current research in biology education in relation to instructional frameworks, intended learning and knowledge acquisition in biology, instructional strategies in biology, student motivation, and transfer of knowledge, retention of knowledge, and student diversity and lesson planning for all students. Based on a critical examination of the research of Sampson and Gerbino (2010), it is clear that changing the approach to biology instruction might support a learning environment that fits well with the nature of science and new pedagogical content knowledge in biology. Creating an environment that allows all students to learn science is critical. The active participation of students can improve student achievement in biology. As Sampson and Gerbino noted, students need to know how new knowledge is generated and validated by scientists as well as the important theories, laws, and unifying concepts of the various disciplines in order to understand science as a way of knowing. Students also must develop the abilities and habits of mind needed to construct and support scientific claims through argument and to evaluate or challenge the claims or arguments developed by others. (p. 427)

In addition, active participation of students and positive perceptions of teachers about their students can improve student motivation to learn in biology classrooms. According to Watters and Watters (2007), science education should also focus on pedagogical skills and the competencies of the teacher. Thus, section VI also informs this application section. Both sections V and VI support the argument that attention to student needs, the use of exemplary instructional strategies, an emphasis on meeting the learning needs of a diverse student group, and quality lesson planning can serve as a strong base for improving science education and as instruments for effecting positive social change in today's fast growing technological society.

The purpose of this application section is to describe a professional development session in relation to providing science teachers with guidance in using different instructional strategies that are informed by theories of a learning organization. This professional development session was delivered to science instructors at Any High School USA, through a Power Point Presentation that included discussion and hands-on activities. This narrative includes the rationale behind the session, the justification for elements of the session design, and a conclusion explaining how the theories of the previous sections can be put into practice.

Project Rationale

This professional development session was an effort to help science teachers to reach and serve a generation of students who are fundamentally different than those who came before them. Lee and Buxton (2008) pointed out that "students in today's classroom are much more diverse than yesterday's student" (p. 124). Based on literature about high-stakes testing and accountability in science education, which has demanded an even more robust science curriculum, many students are still considered latecomers in the science field. If that is the case, then teachers have to work to eliminate the complexities of science education. This complexity in science education currently requires students to possess a conceptual understanding of other sciences such as physics and chemistry as well as mathematics. Thus, this application project is meant to help teachers become aware of this complexity and to help them resolve the problem. The hope is that teachers might change their teaching styles by incorporating certain instructional strategies in order to help students improve their learning.

Project Design

The professional development session began with the instructor welcoming participants and introducing himself, his role as educational consultant. After the introduction, several minutes were spent on an opening anecdote, participant introductions, and related discussion. In an effort to connect the content of the session with the participants' lives, both professional and personal, the presenter shared an anecdote about his experiences as a biology student and teacher. Participants were then asked to introduce themselves and to share (in addition to their name, classroom location, and grade or science subject taught) one hope for the future of science education and what role they might play in the improvement of science education. After participants shared their ideas, the presenter led a discussion related to instructional issues. During this discussion, many of the concepts evident in Sections V and VI surfaced.

Following the opening discussion, the formal content was introduced, beginning with a review of current trends in science education and the current expectations for science educators. This presentation included a review of some of the teaching and learning concepts proposed by Hoy and Miskel (1978). These concepts were explicitly related to the improvement of student achievement through a discussion of the contemporary contributions of Love, (2010); Sampson and Gerbino (2010); Lee and Buxton (2008); and Watters and Watters (2007). This review was followed by an overview of the new material from these sections. Based on the research from the section V portion, participants were introduced to the organizational learning theories of Senge (2006), Hoy and Miskel (1978) and Wheatley (1999). In addition to the work of these theorists, the research of Sampson and Gerbino on instructional strategies in biology and the work of Lee and Buxton (2008) on an instructional framework for equitable learning opportunities were addressed.

Following the overview, a more in-depth discussion of each theorist began. Participants were asked to recall and share their prior knowledge of Senge (2006), and many participants were able to share significant information. The presenter then focused on Senge's belief that a successful organization is an organization that never stops learning; he called these organizations "a learning community" and noted that education should be as much like a learning community as possible in order to be most effective. Following a discussion of organizational development, the presenter also focused on Wheatley's (1999) concept of education as a living system, capable of evolving. The presenter also pointed out Hoy and Miskel's (1978) dedication to improving school organizational systems in order to discover practices that are more effective rather than continuing in what is considered by some as a medieval educational system. Throughout the discussion of Hoy and Miskel's concepts, participants drew parallels about classroom instructional practice as a teacher with when they were students. The discussion of Hoy and Miskel's work transitioned into a more in-depth discussion of Wheatley's concepts, and the participants suggested that if Senge's idea of an organization is a learning community and Wheatley considers an organization as a living system capable of evolving, then education must be a living system, which is constantly learning as well.

Participants were unfamiliar with Wheatley's (1999) beliefs regarding organization as a living system, so her concepts of systems were covered as well. However, participants were familiar with organizations as a learning community (Senge, 2006), so discussion focused on its relevance and application in improving student achievement in science. Having covered so many elements of organizational theory already, the discussion of Hoy and Miskel's (1978) concepts of systems thinking was comparatively brief. Still, participants were introduced to their theory of educational management and bureaucracy and the ways in which they formalized education management strategies. At this point, the presentation turned away from discussing specific theorists from section V to discussion of the current research studies that were examined in the section VI. This discussion began with a brief overview of an instructional framework and instructional strategies for science (Sampson & Gerbino, 2010). Prioritization seemed to be the key word that resonated during the discussion. The presenter asked three questions:

1. What is the correlation between science achievement and improvement in student learning?
2. What does the student believe about science learning?
3. What is an instructional strategy?

Following the presentation of these questions, a discussion was conducted about the role that teachers could play in motivating student to learn science. The majority of the teachers seemed to accept changes to instruction as one of the major ways to improve student motivation. In particular, the discussion focused on the project approach (Watters & Watters, 2007). The presenter shared the advantages and disadvantages of the project approach and asked teachers to come up with ways to use this instructional technique in their classrooms. The presenter encouraged teachers to collaborate across content areas if they wished to use the project approach. Although this section was not included in earlier in the sections, participants were still exposed to issues related to curriculum organization, student engagement, instructional challenges, and rewards that parents and the community might bring to formal education (Posner, 2004). The main point of this portion of the presentation, though, was the discussion about how to use strategic planning to improve science learning. Strategies that parents and community members might use to effect positive social change was discussed and participants were reminded of the social change agenda in science education, influenced by current demands in new technologies. Discussion then moved beyond these changes to other work that is being done in relation to improving science education in general.

Participants were also introduced to the research of Sampson and Gerbino (2010) on scientific argument. One of Sampson and Gerbino's journal articles was distributed for participants to read and share. This distribution was followed by discussion of an instructional strategy that could be used in relation to the human lymphatic system. Time was allocated to complete a model lesson, and responses were reviewed for discussion.

This discussion was approximately 45 minutes, which was followed by a 10-minute break. Then a PowerPoint Presentation was used to discuss instructional strategies with participants. After this presentation, a model instructional lesson in biology was presented titled *Lymphatic Systems and Body Defenses*. This introductory lesson was followed by a lecture created by Sampson and Gerbino (2010).

The "generate-an-argument" instructional strategy was also shared; participants were informed that this strategy was designed to engage students in scientific argumentation without gathering data in the lab. The objective was for students to generate a claim that answers a scientific question based on current or historical scientific data, develop a reasonable argument, and respond to critical comments from others (Sampson & Gerbino, 2010). The presenter of this professional development activity was not a participant. He monitored each group, offering assistance, and clarifying questions that teachers asked.

Once the lessons were completed, teachers shared their experiences with the instructional strategy. The teachers were asked to stay in their groups. Each group was given a large poster upon which to record their experiences. Participant from each group were allowed to share their discussion, using the following prepared questions:

1. What counts as an argument in science?
2. How did the enthusiasm and motivation differ among participants?
3. What were some comments from the participants?
4. What are ways that this instructional strategy can be adapted to your classroom?

During the sharing session, there were several comments, laughter, and facial and body expressions that seemed to come from the lesson activities. It seemed that the majority of the teachers who participated in this activity could visualize parallels between the professional development and instruction in their classrooms. Participants were asked to discuss what they observed. The majority of the teachers noted that listening to each group listening and asking questions allowed them to stay focused and motivated. The physics teacher explained that the lesson made him think about the students in his class. The consensus was that the strategy will prevent student boredom that currently exists in science classes.

If time permitted, a final discussion session was planned. Participants were to use the think-pair-share strategy to consider possible uses for different instructional strategies in their classrooms. Each teacher would think about the question individually, then discuss it with a partner, and finally share it with the group. Following this activity, they would be invited to brainstorm lesson plans using these ideas. When the session was implemented, time limitations dictated that the presenter move ahead to the final reflection questions, in which participants were asked to reevaluate their answers to the questions posed during the introduction. Participants were then asked what their next steps might be before the session was brought to a close with a final evaluation.

In the final evaluation, 100% of the participants strongly agreed that the presenter demonstrated knowledge of the subject matter and was well prepared and organized. One hundred percent also agreed or strongly agreed that the presenter was able to stimulate interest and respond to participants needs. Several participants left enthusiastic positive comments such as "Great class! Good resources!" and "The presenter was very knowledgeable about the subject matter. Thank you for your time! I enjoyed the presentation!"

When asked how the session could have been improved, some participants shared constructive suggestions as well. Following are some samples. One teacher stated, "I would love to attend an in-service that would give me information specifically for collaboration with mathematics teachers". Another teacher commented, "Many of the strategies were more of collaboration between science and English Language Arts". Another teacher also noted, "My students are mostly English learners; I see the benefit of the writing and speaking part". One teacher commented, "I would have enjoyed more time to actually explore different instructional strategies in science more, rather than learning about the theorists and those people that developed the original ideas". Another teacher remarked, "I probably won't remember the names of all the theorists, but if there were a chance to learn by going online to their websites or something that would be a little more interesting. I would enjoy more ideas to take home and research or implement."

This session may be offered again as an on-going professional development for science teachers, and emphasis would be focused on the use of effective and efficient instructional strategies and delivery in science lessons. The feedback from participant evaluations will be valuable in the presenter's effort to improve the session for these future events.

Theory to Practice

Section V described theories and concepts related to organizational development, with a focus on the works of Senge, Wheatley, and Hoy and Miskel. These concepts were put into practice through this application portion of the paper in a professional development session. Participants might now apply these concepts about organizational development to their teaching and to their own awareness, experience, and imagination in the science courses they teach.

Section VI was a critical examination of current research related to science education, including such concepts as instructional frameworks, intended learning and knowledge acquisition, instructional strategies in science, student motivation, transfer of knowledge, retention of knowledge, student diversity, and lesson planning in relation to theories and concepts about organizational development that were described in the breadth section. Participants were given the opportunity to apply the research studies of Sampson and Gerbino (2010), Watters and Watters (2007), and Cook (2010) in their own classes. Along with section V and VI portions of this paper, the application portion also supported the argument that performance based learning (PBL) and teacher pedagogical content knowledge (PCK) can serve as strategic learning tools and as instruments for effecting biology teaching in high schools. This application portion also provided participants with a hands-on segment; teachers were able to experience and reflect on the role of these theories and concepts in practice. Finally, participants were introduced to a variety of ways to apply these theories and concepts in their own classrooms, including the use of cooperative learning, equitable learning opportunities, and role-playing. Ultimately, the focus was on the potential power of PBL and PCK to serve as instructional learning tools and as instruments for science education. The hope is that participants will indeed apply these theories in their own roles as science educators and thus ensure that students are prepared for the challenge of science.

Student active participation during instruction and teacher's positive perceptions of all students did show to motivate and increase students' learning in biology class. The application section was presented to provide a professional development (PD) experience for science teachers on different instructional strategies available in science instructions. The professional development was delivered by a

Power Point Presentation; started with discussion of current and future issues facing science education. Participants were allowed to share ideas and evaluate different thoughts on science education from other participants.

Included with the narratives was the rationale behind the project, the design, and the justification of the session. In the rationale part of the project, the knowledge that k-12 school system are charged to teach and meet the needs of all students regardless of race and mental capability; the same can be said for biology course. Thus, the rationale here is to use this professional development and create awareness among science teachers in order to change or incorporate different teaching strategies. The change in instructional strategy will reduce the complexities that made science challenging for many students.

In the project design, the presenter started by introducing his experience as a biology student and teacher, and then allowed participants to share their experiences as a student and a teacher. The next discussion was shifted to the work of the theorists presented in the section V followed by the current research in biological instructional techniques. The presenter made connections between the theorists' work and social systems and the current studies in biological instructions. After discussing the theorists from section V and section VI, the presenter then delivered a modeled teaching technique for the participants. In the section of theory to practice, the presenter made several connections between the Sections V and VI using examples and modeled lesson plan.

Systems thinking were integrated from the principles of Peter Senge, Hoy & Miskel., and Margaret Wheatley, with assistance from contemporary use of their concepts, to examine the context biology instruction. Undertaking the application of these concepts perspective, could make significant contributions towards student achievement in biology.

REFERENCES

Aoki, J. M., Foster, A. S., & Ramsey, J. M. (2005). Inquiry perceptions held by responding Greater Houston-area science supervisors. *Texas Science Teacher, 34*(2), 17-22.

Campbell, T., & Bohn, C. (2008). Science laboratory experiences of high school students across one State in the U.S.: descriptive research from the classroom. *Science Educator, 17*(1), 36-48.

Campbell, T., Oh, P.S., Shin, M.K., & Zhang, D. (2010). Classroom instructions observed from the perspectives of current reform in science education: Comparisons between korean and U.S. classrooms. *Eurasia Journal of Mathematics, Science & Technology Education, 6*(3), 151-162.

Caravita, S., Valente, A., Luzi, D., Pace, P., Valanides, N., Khalil, I., & Clément, P. (2008).Construction and validation of textbook analysis grids for ecology and environmental education. *Science Education International, 19*(2), 97-116.

Childs, A., & McNicholl, J. (2007). Science teachers teaching outside of subject specialism: challenges, strategies adopted and implications for initial eacher education. *Teacher Development, 11*(1), 1-20.

Cook, K. (2009). A suggested project-based evolution unit for high school: Teaching content through application. *American Biology Teacher, 71*(2), 95-98.

Costa, A.L, & Garmston, R. J. (2002). *Cognitive coaching: a foundation for renaissance schools* (2nd ed.). Norwood, MA: Christopher-Gordon.

Ellis, E. S., & Worthington, L. A. (1994). *Research synthesis on effective teaching principles and the design of quality tools for educators.* (Tech. Rep. No. 5). Eugene, OR: National Center to Improve the Tools of Educators. (ERIC Document Reproduction Service No. ED386853). Retrieve February 7, 2011 from http://www.eric.ed.gov.

Gioka, O. (2009). Teacher or examiner? The tensions between formative and summative assessment in the case of science coursework. *Research in Science Education, 39*(4), 411-428.

Gredler, M.E. (2009). *Learning and instruction: theory into practice* (6th ed.). Upper Saddle River, NJ: Pearson.

Hochberg, R., & Gabric, K. (2010). A provably necessary symbiosis. *American Biology Teacher, 72*(5), 296-300.

Huitt, W. (2001). Motivation to learn: an overview. *Educational Psychology Interactive.* Valdosta, GA: Valdosta state University. Retrieved January 17, 2011, from www.edpsycinteractive.org/col/motivation/motivate.html

Hunt, G.H; Wiseman, D.G and Touzel, T.M. (2009). *Effective teaching: preparation and implementation* (4th ed.). Springfield, IL: Charles C Thomas.

Hunter, R. (2004). *Mastery teaching: increasing instructional effectiveness in elementary and secondary schools.* Thousand Oaks, CA: Sage.

Kin Hang Wong, K., & Day, J. (2009). A comparative study of problem-based and lecture-based learning in junior secondary school science. *Research in Science Education, 39*(5), 625-642.

Lee, O., & Buxton, C. (2008). Science curriculum and student diversity: a framework for equitable learning opportunities. *Elementary School Journal, 109*(2), 123-137.

Lee, E. and Loft, J.A. (2008). Experience secondary science teachers' representation of pedagogical content knowledge. *Instructional Journal of Science Education, 30*(4), 1343-1363

Lord, T., & Orkwiszewski, T. (2006). Moving from didactic to inquiry-based instruction in a science laboratory. *The American Biology Teacher, 68*(6), 342-345.

Lotter, C., Singer, J., & Godley, J. (2009). The influence of repeated teaching and reflection on preservice teachers' views of inquiry and nature of science. *Journal of Science Teacher Education, 20*(6), 553-582.

Love, A. C. (2010). Darwin's "Imaginary Illustrations": Creatively teaching evolutionary concepts & the nature of science. *American Biology Teacher, 72*(2), 82-89.

Marieb, E. (2003). *Essentials of human anatomy and physiology.* (7th ed.). San Francisco, Benjamin Cummings.

Marzano, R.J., Pickering, J.D., & Pollock, J.E. (2001). *Classroom instruction that works: research based strategies for increasing student achievement.* Alexandria, VA: Association for supervision and curriculum development.

Mualem, R., & Eylon, B. (2009). Teaching physics in junior high school: Crossing the borders of fear. *European Journal of Teacher Education, 32*(2), 135-150.

O'Hara, S., & Pritchard, R. H. (2008). Meeting the challenge of diversity: professional development for teacher educators. *Teacher Education Quarterly, 35*(1), 43-61.

Practices and innovations in australian science teacher education programs. *Research in Science Education, 38*(2), 167-188.

Pombo, L., & Costa, N. (2009). The impact of biology/geology school teachers masters courses on the improvement of science education quality in Portugal. *Research in Science & Technological Education, 27*(1), 31-44.

Sampson, V., & Gerbino, F. (2010). Two instructional models that teachers can use to promote & support scientific argumentation in the biology classroom. *American Biology Teacher, 72*(7), 427-431.

Saravia-Shore and Garcia, E. (1992). Diverse teaching strategies for diverse learners. Educating everybody's children, pp. 47-74. Retrieved January 17, 2011 from Xantum course package.

Šorgo, A. (2010). Apacer: A six-step model for the introduction of computer- supported laboratory exercises in biology teaching. *Problems of Education in the 21st Century, 24,* 130-138.

Stephens, K., & Winterbottom, M. (2010). Using a learning log to support students' learning in biology lessons. Journal of Biological Education, *44*(2), 72-80.

Thompson, C. (2009, May). Preparation, practice, and performance An empirical examination of the impact of Standards-based Instruction on secondary students' math and science achievement. *Research in Education, 81,* 53-62.

Watters, D. J., & Watters, J. J. (2007). Approaches to learning by students in the biological sciences: Implications for teaching. *International Journal of Science Education, 29*(1), 19-43.

Withee, T., & Lindell, R. (2006). Different views on inquiry: A survey of science and mathematics methods instructors. *AIP Conference Proceedings, 818*(1), 125-128.

CPSIA information can be obtained
at www.ICGtesting.com
Printed in the USA
LVHW021036180520
655849LV00002B/110